Foreword

(Part 1) Movies:

I was an athletic kid but I hated the idea of playing the same game every day as a job; so unlike most of the kids I grew up with, I never wanted to be an athlete.

I remember my dad asked me once "What do you want to do when you grow up?", to which I absurdly said "I don't know. Maybe I'll play hockey or something".

I said this because I thought "*I mean, I like playing. It's fun*".

Dad knew what it took to become a professional hockey player. Him and my uncles were intense about the game, but my dad knew that there were plenty of people who surpassed him in the necessary desire to become a professional hockey player. My dad's calling was very different and perhaps that was by design.

My dad (being the excellent father he is) told me the honest-to-God truth about the matter and told me flat-out "You don't want to be a hockey player."

I was surprised. I thought he meant "*It's not fun*" or something.

I said "How would you know?"

My dad had a habit of saying things in a very honest (yet not demeaning) tone. It came off as wisdom, unlike most people I've heard try to relay this same message. Unlike people who would say "*You don't have what it takes*" or something inaccurate like that, Dad chose his words with deliberation and candor.

He said "People who want it, and I mean REALLY want it; they go outside and shoot the puck on a net every single day, all day." Dad then followed up with a question that let me dictate my own path in life, rather than letting him choose my life for me.

He asked "To become a professional hockey player, would you do that; every day you can, non-stop?"

I thought about the massive amount of hours, doing the same monotonous thing, every single day. I wanted absolutely nothing to do with it.

I knew myself and knew that I needed to have a new event every day

1

or I'd go crazy. It was not the life for me.

To bring this back to writing; thankfully you dont NEED this obsession to write; just like I didn't need an obsession with hockey in order to casually enjoy the game for the rest of my childhood.

What I mean to say is, don't let this deter you from writing. Believe me, I'd love to see what you make no matter who you are. It's all about the adventure of writing a story. That, and having one person (even just one) who can empathize with your expression; I'm going to tell you from experience; it will mean the world to anyone lucky enough to witness it.

I, on the other hand, found my obsession in filmmaking and writing. It was a never-ending supply of adventure and challenges.

It all began when I saw movies at the Apple Cinemas in Cambridge, MA. I wondered how people made these exhilarating experiences. As a kid, they had me pretending I had claws between my knuckles, and I was hanging upside-down from every part of the playground like I was going to win MTV's Best Kiss Award (look up the winner of 2003 if you don't get the reference).

How could someone come up with such incredible things as movies?

In my old neighborhood (in Somerville) we didn't have a yard to play in. We were told not to run or jump around our home because it annoyed our neighbors downstairs. The local park had a group of alcoholic men on one corner, MS-13 on the other side, and needles sitting in the grass at random.

Because of this, I played a lot of video games before I moved to the suburbs. My cousins introduced me to Mortal Kombat, Armored Core, and many other experiences that would shape my ideas in the future. My father didn't like video games very much, but one odd afternoon we were at BestBuy and he saw a copy of Metal Gear Solid.

He said "This looks cool. I think I'm gonna play it."

My brother and I thought "Dad's joking. He's almost ANTI-videogames, and besides, Dad jokes like that. He SURELY wouldn't play a video game. That's just not possible."

Well, Dad went to the register and bought the game and we thought "Of course he got it for us... He wouldn't..."

When we got home, my dad booted up the Playstation (that he bought with his own damned money, so by God he was gonna play it at

2

least ONCE in his life).

For the next several hours as Dad played, my brother and I were transfixed as he played as Solid Snake and infiltrated Shadow Moses Island to take out the notorious weapon of mass-destruction called "Metal Gear".

I thought I had seen everything there was. At the Apple Cinema, I'd seen toys come to life. On TV, I saw space wizards wield laser swords against one another. I had seen dinosaurs break loose from an island-wide petting zoo and in a sequel, I saw one of those dinosaurs set loose in a city.

How in the world did this team of people from Japan make something unlike anything I'd EVER seen before? I thought I'd seen it all!

It all boiled down to story. How to build one. How to write one. How to maximize the intrigue and deliver an experience unlike any other.

(Part 2) Why publish this book?:

This short book is meant to do two things. One, is to tell a story in a way that is quick, easy, and inexpensive; and if you like what you read, then I look forward to showing you my many other stories in the future.

The second purpose (and in my opinion the more important reason) is to give something to the kid I once was; desperate to figure out *"How do I become a filmmaker?"*.

For now, in this book, we'll be completely focused on the writing part of the process. It's all you can do as a beginner and is the most important part to learn, if you want genuine success.

Side note*

(*It's important to understand something you'll hear a thousand times in Hollywood if you move out here:*

There's a phrase that goes "All you need is a good script", which is true to an extent. A good script is necessary to actually make something people enjoy thoroughly. However, if you're out here you'll see amazing scripts that don't get picked up and terrible scripts that have multiple installations: sequels, prequels, spin-offs and whatever else.

This is a matter of knowing "the ins and outs of legal and business"; because terrible concepts will have their paperwork in order while the "best script ever" will result in a lawsuit if it gets made; but we won't get into that in this book. It's way too advanced for now.)

I was a terrible student in high school but I've made strides both academically and in my achievements as a filmmaker. I've taken part in a Kickstarter campaign that exceeded well beyond its goal. Before the age of twenty-five I made a commercial that aired before a season opening RedSox game. I also directed a series political advertisements that ended in a landslide victory; and all of these achievements were reached before the age of thirty. (*If you're a forty-year old filmmaker who hasn't achieved this, don't worry. I'm sure you know already; some of that success is a matter of sheer circumstantial dumb luck. Don't let other people's accomplishments discourage you. I hate when that happens.*).

I bring all of this up to show just how much my methods have been effective, and nothing more. I don't think I'm special in my abilities, but I've been obsessed with acquiring the skills to do my job as a writer and director. I put my resources and ideas here for you because I selfishly want to see what you make. I love movies and I love watching them. I want you to make something I'll love to see, and we should all feel that way.

Side note*
(*If you work as an artist, you'll notice that each person has their own individual hierarchy of emphasis. One person will prefer to focus on their composition, another will hold their pacing to the highest regard, etc. This results in every individual's "voice". A cliché term used to talk about every person's individual hierarchy. This is what makes everyone different. You don't have competition with your fellow filmmakers, they just make different movies. If you gave the exact same script to Christopher Nolan and Tim Burton, you'd get two completely different movies.*)

(Part 3) Mental Effects:
Why mention that I was a bad high school student?
Well, it serves as proof that it's never too late to change course and learn from your past mistakes. In fact, it did nothing but enhance my confidence to witness my own upward mobility first-hand. Keep in mind, I wasn't aware of this progress as it was happening. It's only been in hindsight that I realized my progress, and for years (*even during my*

4

previously mentioned achievements) I couldn't recognize the progress as it was happening.

The reason I tell you this is to accurately depict what the transition into adulthood will look like for you, and by extension what it will look like to enter a world of professionalism (*as a writer*) because we've all received well intended but inaccurate ideas of writing and filmmaking by people who chose a different path from the one we follow.

(Part 4) "There's only so-and-so many stories.":
Unlike every ding-a-ling who tells you "there are only so-and-so many stories and everything is just a copy of one another" I'm going to tell you that that's an absurd notion. Don't let those people steal your thunder because that's what they're trying to do and there's a reason they haven't made an everlasting experience themselves. It's elephant manure and they know it (*even if they give some decent advise from time to time*).

The truth is, there are certain story-types that have an impressive effect, and we all end up fitting a mold that can closely RESEMBLE these "so-and-so many" stories; but every story is actually different. It took skill to make it happen, not a formula. It took a knowledge of emotional impact and how to conduct the experience that maximized the story's impact.

If everything was just a copy, then everything would be a smash hit. The fact that everything ISN'T a smash hit is only proof that it takes a conductor and not an assembly line. (*Not to say those "copy-paste" romance novels and such don't have a place in this world, but... you know what I mean*).

The point I'm getting at is, people can green light hollow tid-bits of mildly amusing "content" to numb our minds, but all of that is achievable with the algorithm technology we call "*A.I.*". There's nothing intelligent about the bot, and we're ingratiating it with a title reserved for truly sentient technology (*which doesn't exist yet*).

What kind of a life would that be? Living with analytically generated stories? Probably not much better than the analytically curated data we've been green lighting movies and video games with for the past ten years. There's a reason old games and movies still sell better than new ones.

The core principle of any exchange of goods is "*competition*". It takes

5

ingenuity to overcome the competition that's out there, and there's always going to be a love and desire for hand-crafted movies, books, and other media. We will always want a Stephen Spielberg, a J.R.R. Tolkien, or a William Shakespeare. To put it simply, playwrights, authors, and filmmakers will be necessary so long as you don't feel the need to congratulate a robot for beating you at a game of chess. If it can't comprehend its accomplishment or appreciate a "*congratulations*", then it can't understand the emotional conduction of story-craft.

This rant doesn't come from the desperation of an artist losing his place in the world, but it's coming from someone who has an obsession with science in the real world.

My novel "Icarus Dawns" is a six-hundred and six page behemoth that took five years to write, and I spoke extensively with scientists at the cutting edge of research in multiple fields.

Before the release of "Open AI" or "Chat GPT", I knew about the technology that was coming. I didn't fully understand what it looked like, but people like Michio Kaku were talking about it in his books. He's actually the person who mentioned the chess-playing analogy I mentioned earlier, and he's gone more extensively than I can on the subject. In fact, if you're ever curious about the future, just read his latest books. He's always been spot-on (*albeit, the way it FEELS when the technology comes out doesn't match the hype of hearing about it; but that's the case with most things*).

A physicist I spoke to on the subject of these "*A.I.*" had scoffed when I called it "*A.I.*" because in reality, they're what we've been calling "*bots*" up until 2020 or so.

This physicist had told me "This is the third or fourth 'A.I.' revolution I've lived through; and the first time it was graphing calculators".

My whole purpose for telling you this is to let you know for a fact that there's a reason to know story craft. There's still a need for our legwork, and I'd really hate to see an artistic dark-age because some tech companies went wild with their marketing departments. If you feel the need to make stories, please do it but know this first; it will take a tremendous amount of effort to learn.

To be better than an algorithm, you need to think outside the box, like a mad-genius. You need to use your brain to weed out improbabilities and plot holes, but you need your heart to make an effective story. Some stories even forego the brain part and just bend the rules of reality for the greatest narrative effect (*think cartoons or absurdist stories; frequently comedies*).

(Part 5) The Rules:
So what's to be done? How do we learn? What do we do to ensure there's always SOMEBODY raising the bar and giving us something we've never seen before?

Before we get to that, you'll need to know how to read and write a script.

I'll provide a key here, so you'll know what these abbreviations mean:

INT. = Interior
EXT. = Exterior
INT. / EXT. = Interior / Exterior (frequently used for car scenes)
m.o.s. = Without Sound
o.s. = Off Screen
v.o. = Voice Over

The elements of a screenplay will become apparent as you read it. INT. will be followed by a location, then a dash "-" and an expansion on that location (*usually a sub-location within the one that's already been established*).

Another element you'll see is the "parenthetical" (*anything in parentheses... kinda like this!*). That's used for the descriptor of how something is said, however there's a fine line to walk between just telling an actor how to read a line and making sure that you're getting a line across the right way. What do I mean? I mean, don't tell someone how to do their job. They won't appreciate it.

When in doubt, don't tell an actor what to do, but guide them with your skillful use of language. For example, if Todd puts his hand on Deb's shoulder and says "Nice job.", that could be said a thousand ways; but if he SLAPS his hand over her shoulder and says "Nice job!"... well, you didn't throw people off by saying "Todd: (boisterous) 'Nice job!'". If you read the two side-by-side, one is jarring while the other glides you along through the story, and you won't even realize you were swayed to read it in a certain way.

We'll get into details like that after the script portion of this book, but it's important to know why you'll see a parenthetical in select circum-

7

stances and not all over the place.

You'll also notice there are some very percussive moments and quick paragraph changes for high action sequences. A script doesn't have the page space to describe things the way a novel does. Not only that, but we try to alleviate the psychological burden of ink, leaving as much blank space as possible to keep our reader invested and flowing with the story. Writing in this fashion makes reading our work feel like we're watching the events play out on a screen.

Moments like: "CRASH! He tumbles into a dresser!" followed by a line break and the next action (*a punch or a kick or something*); it's necessary for us to get the idea in as few words as possible. Not only that, but actions like this take up time that is determined by a film's on-set shooting (*production*) and the editor's choice of how long he'll hold the shot for (*post-production*). The end result frequently gives each action as much time and narrative weight as a line of dialogue. The result is

Quick

Lines

That break.

So now that you know that there's a reason to learn story craft (*that we won't be replaced by bots*), and now that you know how to read a script, let's take a look at the story. Shall we?

About the story:

This story was conceived in 2011, and was made at a time when I had no resources on how to write. It's been living in my head for almost a decade and a half, and it's progressed into an enhanced version of its original form.

The original story had no clear path and now that I've learned my craft, I've finally put it to paper for you to read.

After the story is over, I'll give you the direction I desired back then and hopefully you can start your journey to become a writer.

Tears of Anemoia

By Erik James Troy

EXT. BACK WOODS UNDER A TRAIN BRIDGE - NEW EN-
GLAND TOWN - DAY

Overcast. An early spring day. A HOMELESS MAN
struggles to nestle himself in a place out of
sight.

OTHER HOMELESS can be heard close by skulking
their way over the bridge, seeking a fix of what
he has.

Their footsteps and voices travel above, across
the bridge, and fade to a mere echo the woods.

He unfurls a baggie. A spoon, and a lighter.

Just one more check, and the coast is clear. He
injects himself.

He's high. His vision is blurry, and the world
spins.

A HOODED MAN appears on the other side of the
train bridge. It's like he was waiting. The
Homeless Man can hear his own heart thump in
his ears.

The hooded man crosses the stream. He's closer with each glimpse. The homeless man can only
watch. His legs melt and his hands lap the
boulders around him as he tries to crawl away.

He turns on his side and there's the hooded man
standing above him. The homeless man almost
gives in, but he comes to his senses, and his
eyes widen in horror.

The hooded man holds the homeless man's guts in
his hands. He licks the entrails like it's ice
cream on a cone.

Then, the hooded man grabs the homeless man's
head and pulls it from his body.

It tumbles to the floor so that the homeless man
can see his blood spewing from his body, and

the hooded man cupping his hands. He sips from
the pool between his fingers.

The homeless man's vision fades.

EXT. DUGOUT - ANDOVER HIGH SCHOOL - DAY

OLIVIA sits with four other GIRLS who smoke
weed near her. They pass a bowl around. Olivia
abstains.

                    GIRL 1
          She left with her
          thirty-year-old boy-
          friend.

                    GIRL 2
          Sketch Dan?

                    GIRL 3
          Sketch Dan was at
          Brother's yesterday.
          If she ran away, it
          wasn't with him.-

                    GIRL 1
          Do you think he killed
          her?

                    GIRL 2
          A lover's quarrel or
          whatever-

The girls cackle and snort at Girl 2's proper
English.

Olivia sees THREE BOYS lumber toward the dugout. Her ex boyfriend JAKE is one of them.

                    GIRL 1
          Oh shit!

Olivia wrenches her bag to leave. Girl 3 helps
her gather her phone and other belongings.

                         GIRL 2
                    Run girl! Run!

The girls obstruct the sight of Olivia's exit
with a wall of their bodies, peacocking and
primping; almost all of it a charade to dis-
tract the boys.

INT. OLIVIA'S HOUSE - FRONT DOOR - LATER

OLIVIA slides her bag from her shoulders and it
thumps to the ground.

She hauls her homework out and picks up a granola bar from a bowl on the counter.

A pitter-patter grabs her attention. Her dog
(PIGEON) waddles in with his bed-head. She
gives him a proper greeting.

She fills his bowl with food, then rips into her
granola bar with her teeth. She moves back to
her books with a wide-split stance.

                         OLIVIA
                    I do NOT want to deal
                    with your shit later.
                    You are getting done
                    NOW.

She sticks her erect finger at the open pages of
her textbook.

                         OLIVIA
                    You're goin' down!

INT. OLIVIA'S HOUSE - LIVING ROOM - LATER

The textbook slams onto the coffee table. OLIV-
IA drops onto the couch and writes in her notebook.

                         OLIVIA
                    Forty-two. Easy.

She tosses her notebook like a frisbee and it

                           12

slaps on the table. She launches herself up to look for her trumpet.

INT. OLIVIA'S HOUSE - OFFICE - LATER

OLIVIA reads her Facebook feed (2011 Facebook) as the dial-tone rings for her mother on speakerphone.

The Facebook feed is loaded with comments on a girl named Ashley's profile. The comments say "Where are you?" and "I miss you so much".

A "Town Moms" group shows a "Missing Person" post about her.

                    PATRICIA
                    (o.s.)
            Hello?

                    OLIVIA
            Hey.

Olivia treats this as a chat with her mother, but her MOTHER is overworked and demands respect in Olivia's tone.

                    PATRICIA
                    (o.s.)
            Well "hey" to you TOO!

                    OLIVIA
            When are you getting
            home?

Olivia's mother stops herself from venting on her daughter who just wants to chat.

                    PATRICIA
                    (o.s.)
            I have a few more pa-
            tients to see; then
            I'm out and on vay-
            cay.

                    OLIVIA
          Jeez Mom, the man pro-
          posed to you. He spent
          his hard earned money
          on a diamond ring, and
          you have the AUDACITY,
          nay, the GALL-!

Olivia's mother doesn't have time for her
daughter's sarcasm.

                    PATRICIA
                    (o.s.)
          Olivia, what are you
          getting at?

                    OLIVIA
          It's your honeymoon,
          Mom. Aren't you excit-
          ed?

                    PATRICIA
                    (o.s.)
          When you get to my
          age, it's no big deal.

                    OLIVIA
          Yeah you should get
          REAL pessimistic and
          just start calling
          this "round two"!

                    PATRICIA
                    (o.s.)
          Olivia.

Olivia smiles to herself and logs out of Facebook. She then lays on some more sarcasm and
makes demands.

                    OLIVIA
          Get home. I want qual-
          ity time. In fact, I
          demand it.

                    PATRICIA
                    (o.s.)
            Alright. I'll see you
            soon.

INT. OLIVIA'S HOUSE - LIVING ROOM - NIGHT

OLIVIA lulls some notes on her trumpet while
she stares off in thought on the sofa. Her
phone is on speaker with Girl 3.

                    GIRL 3
                    (o.s.)
            He DID ask about you,
            but I don't know if
            that's a good thing.

                    OLIVIA
            Not the best.

                    GIRL 3
                    (o.s.)
            Well he's cute so-
            even if you don't want
            him, it's nice that he
            wants you.

Keys clang and tinkle. The front door unlocks.

                    OLIVIA
            I'd rather that he'd
            just move on. Hey lis-
            ten, I've gotta go. My
            mom's home.

                    GIRL 3
                    (o.s.)
            Tell your mom I say
            "hi"!

                    OLIVIA
            Will do.

INT. OLIVIA'S HOUSE - FRONT DOOR - CONTINUOUS

OLIVIA'S MOTHER lumbers into the house, laden

with groceries.

                    OLIVIA
          You're late.

                    PATRICIA
          I'm too tired for
          this. Come on and give
          me a hand.

OLIVIA lends her help.

                    OLIVIA
          The heck happened?

                    PATRICIA
          A five year old with
          cancer, Olivia. Don't
          you give me grief.
          Okay? Back off.

                    OLIVIA
          No grief, Mom. Relax.

They step outside to grab more bags.

EXT. OLIVIA'S HOUSE - DRIVEWAY - NIGHT

Olivia's mother (PATRICIA) yanks bags from the
back of the car.

                    OLIVIA
          No movie tonight?

                    PATRICIA
          I'm sorry honey. I
          can't. I have the day
          off tomorrow. -Have
          you called your father
          yet?

OLIVIA makes a face that says she didn't.

                    PATRICIA
          Damn it, Olivia.

                    OLIVIA
          Mom, he's kinda sad to
          look at. It just makes
          me-

                    PATRICIA
          You won't have that
          BOY coming over!

                    OLIVIA
          I broke it off with
          Jake a while ago. He's
          not coming near the
          house.

                    PATRICIA
          Well you're spending
          time with your father.
          I can't be the only-

An old lady (MRS. KRAFTON) hobbles up the
driveway with a small flashlight.

                    PATRICIA
          Hey Mrs. Krafton!

                    MRS. KRAFTON
          Hello darlin'!

                    OLIVIA
          Hey Mrs. K!

                    MRS. KRAFTON
          Olivia, honey. Could
          you do me a favor?

                    OLIVIA
          Anything you need Mrs.
          K.

                    MRS. KRAFTON
          You play the trumpet
          so beautifully. I re-
          ally enjoy it, even
          though I can't hear
          very well anymore. You

                        17

see, my Spike can hear
it, and he has a hard
time sleeping; and
well, he's a big dog
you see.

           PATRICIA
Was Olivia playing
late? I told you not
to do that-

      MRS. KRAFTON
I was just wondering
if after eight P.M.
you might-.

           OLIVIA
Of course, Mrs. Kraf-
ton. I'm sorry.
Spike's a good boy
and he deserves a
good night's sleep.
-I mean, you should
see how I get when I
don't get a full eight
hours.

      MRS. KRAFTON
Oh nonsense, dear.
You're always at a
hundred percent. And
to be honest, your
mother's twenty per-
cent looks better than
most people's hundred.

           PATRICIA
Oh Mrs. Krafton, thank
you!

      MRS. KRAFTON
Don't mention it!
I'm only telling the
truth. And that's good
news for you, Olivia.
You'll be running on

all cylinders even at
my age.

                PATRICIA
          Well you're doing
          great Mrs. Krafton.

                MRS. KRAFTON
          What do ya think?
          Should I try my hand
          at a couple young ones
          down the pub?

The ladies laugh.

                MRS. KRAFTON
          I'm only playin'. You
          ladies have a good
          night. It was nice
          seein' ya.

They say their goodbyes to their neighbor as
she hobbles back into the night.

EXT. PARKING LOT - NIGHT

A GUY is on the phone, smoking a cigarette.

                GUY
          Yeah, I know; but,
          what else can you
          do?- No, Ma' I quit
          smoking. You can tell
          Dad I'm fine.- Al-
          right, well I'll see
          you tomorrow. My flight
          leaves at six in the
          morning.- Okay, love
          you too. Bye.

He throws his cigarette at the ground and
stomps it out. He unlocks his car and pops two
pieces of gum out of a pack.

A woman's scream rips through the air. It
echoes from a void within the woods.

The guy locks his car. He looks closer into the shadows of the forest.

                    GUY
          Hello?

He's alert from the sound but hesitant.

He doesn't know what to do.

The woman's voice whimpers another sentence; hopeless for a reply.

                    WOMAN'S VOICE
          Help me.-

He feels a pit in his stomach and decides to act on instinct. He moves closer to the woods.

INT. OLIVIA'S HOUSE - OLIVIA'S ROOM - MORNING

OLIVIA raises a shirt to her chest, deciding what to wear. Her mother is on the phone with her father, elsewhere in the house.

                    PATRICIA
                    (o.s.)
          -Well, she's dat-
          ing boys as stupid as
          YOU now!- Yeah, that
          perked you up REAL
          quick!

Olivia is aghast at her mother, trying to fight a laugh. PIGEON, on the other hand, is upset, and curled on the bed.

Olivia scratches his ears.

                    OLIVIA
          At least she's funny
          about it.

                    PATRICIA
                    (o.s.)
          She's not gonna want

to do that.- You're one to talk Big Head! I KNOW she won't. I've actually been here in her life; but it can't always be me. You have to step in when I can't and this is one of those moments.

Olivia sympathizes with Pigeon. The longing for a whole family creeps back in, but she shoves that feeling away as usual, and perks up.

She gives Pigeon some belly rubs, then continues getting dressed.

                    PATRICIA
                     (o.s.)
          - Yeah, good luck.
          I won't say a word.
          Watch, she's gonna say
          "no".- Lionel, this
          would not be the first
          time you made a gamble
          and lost, BIG GUY.-
          That wasn't a compli-
          ment!

Olivia smirks at this last part.

INT. ANDOVER HIGH SCHOOL - HALLWAY - DAY

OLIVIA is outside her class when her phone buzzes. It's her father. She moves into the hall to speak with him.

                    OLIVIA
          Hello?

                    LIONEL
                     (o.s.)
          How's my baby girl?

Olivia rushes him, expecting platitudes.

21

                    OLIVIA
          Hey Dad.

                    LIONEL
                    (o.s.)
          Listen, I know you're
          busy at school right
          now, so I won't keep
          you.

Olivia knows he wants to make it brief for his
own reasons.

                    LIONEL
          I wanted to propose an
          idea.- Since your mom
          is out of town, why
          don't you join me in
          Europe for the week?

                    OLIVIA
          Uh. I think I'm good.

                    LIONEL
                    (o.s.)
          What? Honey you'd love
          it! I-

                    OLIVIA
          Dad, I don't wanna be
          stuck in a hotel wait-
          ing for you to finish
          some meeting. God for-
          bid I need to meet a
          French model you're
          dating for the week-
          end.

                    LIONEL
                    (o.s.)
          Chantelle is actually
          gonna be out of town
          this week. That's why
          I wanted to go with
          you now. If I-

JAKE is approaching from the other end of the hall. Olivia becomes hurried.

                    OLIVIA
          Dad, I hate to be
          rude, but I need to
          get to class. Look,
          I'd rather we go ice
          skating or something.
          Remember that time we
          went when I was lit-
          tle?

                    LIONEL
               (o.s.)
          What better place to
          go skating than Swit-
          zerland!

                    OLIVIA
          Dad, this isn't about
          you, this is about
          us.- I know you'd
          rather spend money on
          a trip that feels like
          a vacation to you, but
          a vacation to me is
          just seeing you; or
          not! At this rate it
          doesn't matter. I've
          gotta go. Bye.

Olivia slaps her phone shut, but her way to class is in Jake's path. She leans against a locker, toward the shelter of conversation with another student.

Holding books with both her arms, it's an obo player named KAYLI who happens to be at this locker. She has the air of an Orthodox Catholic girl.

                    OLIVIA
          Hey Kayli. How's obo?

                    KAYLI
          Oh! Olivia! It's been
          good. Are you playing
          trumpet in the summer
          concert this year?

                    OLIVIA
          I don't play much any-
          more. I might be a
          little rusty but we'll
          see.

Jake keeps his eyes away from their direction,
but he has a hard time pretending not to notice
them.

                    KAYLI
          You were a pleasure to
          listen to. I think you
          should do it.

                    OLIVIA
          Thanks.

She looks at Kayli's decorated locker with
glitter and ribbons. It's spangled with pic-
tures of One Direction and Kayli and friends in
photo booths.

                    OLIVIA
          Uh, Kayli?

                    KAYLI
          Yeah?

                    OLIVIA
          I just realized,
          you're the only person
          I've seen use a locker
          in this school. Why?

Kayli's smacks the locker like a proud father
showing off his six-speed mid-life-crisis.

                    KAYLI
          She it helps me stay

                      24

organized. It's my
very own personal bub-
ble over here.

                    OLIVIA
          Interesting. Well
          thank God you do. I
          almost had an embar-
          rassing interaction
          with my ex.

                    KAYLI
          Oh, that's why you
          came out of nowhere!
          Man, and just when I
          thought you were hit-
          ting on me.

Olivia takes a second glance at Kayli who
blushes in a wide grin. Her laughter spills out
in pangs. Her words slipped out in deadpan.

Olivia reads the intent on Kayli's face, and
she's glad that the oboist has shown her funny
side. She laughs with her.

                    OLIVIA
          Well thank you, Kayli.

                    KAYLI
          Of course! I'll always
          be here with my trusty
          ol' locker if you need
          me.

She smacks the locker again with the same
smile.

INT. MARKET BASKET - STORE FRONT - LATER

OLIVIA is on the phone with her mother as she
walks with her employee uniform toward the back
of the store.

                    PATRICIA
                      (o.s.)
          My flight is early in
          the morning. I can
          maybe spare an hour
          or two. Bart will be
          there to pick me up at
          seven.

                    OLIVIA
          Okay; and mom, we
          don't have to watch a
          movie together if you
          don't have the time
          for it. It's okay.

                    PATRICIA
          I said I'd do it, and
          goddamnit, I want to.

                    OLIVIA
          Okay; it's just, I'm
          gonna miss you and
          all, but I don't want
          you to stress. Just
          have fun and don't
          worry about me.

                    PATRICIA
                      (o.s.)
          It's not YOU I'm wor-
          ried about, you see.
          It's your father who
          better-

                    OLIVIA
          He'll be fine, Mom.
          He's gonna stop by,
          we'll spend some qual-
          ity time; no big deal.
          Just relax and have
          fun. I've gotta go,
          Mom. I'm at work. Love
          you.

INT. MARKET BASKET - BACK OF STORE - LATER

                        26

OLIVIA is in the middle of her work day manag-
ing the shelves in the back of the store.

An EMPLOYEE approaches Olivia with a pair of
trash bags; like a five-year-old waiting to ask
his parents for permission.

                    EMPLOYEE
          Olivia?

                    OLIVIA
          Hey! What's up?

                    EMPLOYEE
          Would you take these
          trash bags out to the
          dumpster? It's raining
          out, and I don't want
          to get my hair wet.

Olivia looks at the man's short hair and wonders what the hell he means.

                    OLIVIA
          Uh- Sure! Yeah. After
          all, I heard Sicily
          might be stopping by
          today.

The employee smiles like a cartoon character in
love.

                    OLIVIA
          If you wouldn't mind
          just taking over here
          for me?

The employee begins organizing the shelf.

EXT. BEHIND THE MARKET BASKET - CONTINUOUS

OLIVIA suspends the trash bags in either hand
as she strides toward the dumpster.

At the edge of the woods, behind the Market
Basket, there stands a HOODED MAN, watching

her. Skulking. Prepared to advance.

Olivia watches him from the corner of her eye; pressing her luck by going to the dumpster and closing the gap between them. She stops and tries to shame him away by scolding.

                    OLIVIA
          Can I help you, sir?

The man doesn't say a word. She's frightened but still tries her luck and moves forward, keeping an eye on him the whole way.

She throws the first bag. The man breaks into a full sprint! She drops the other bag! She runs!

A hand grabs her at the waist!

He spins her around!

She's off her feet.

He holds her arm and neck against the wall.

Her back scrapes on the brick behind her.

She's pained and tries to fight.

He sniffs around her body.

She would scream if she could, but his hand has moved onto her mouth. She can only watch without any means to fight or scream.

He continues to smell her.

The hooded man pauses, and his grip slackens.

He lets go. She drops to the ground and he vanishes.

Olivia catches her footing and looks up toward the woods.
There's no sign of the hooded man.

INT. MARKET BASKET - BACK OF STORE - CONTINUOUS

OLIVIA comes inside. She ignores the EMPLOYEE
with his dry buzzcut.

She gets into a quiet place to call her mother.

The phone rings, but her mother doesn't pick
up. A voicemail plays.

                    PATRICIA
                     (v.o.)
            Hello, you've reached
            Patricia. I'm off on
            vacation for the week-
            end, so please bear
            with me while I'm
            away. I'll get back to
            you as soon as I've
            had some well needed
            rest and relaxation.
            Bye!

The voicemail beeps and Olivia stumbles on her
words.

                    OLIVIA
            Hey mom.- I wanted
            to call and see what
            movie you wanted to
            watch. That's all.-
            Love you, bye.

Olivia claps the phone shut, then looks at herself in a mirror. She trying her best to calm
herself down.

EXT. ANDOVER WOODS - CONTINUOUS

The HOODED MAN rasps and gasps; shaking. His
nails are covered in dirt while he looks at his
hands.

He looks either way, then listens and smells
the air.

EXT. ANDOVER WOODS - ELSEWHERE - CONTINUOUS

A DEER looks for acorns under the leaves and branches of the forest floor.

The HOODED MAN watches from a distance.

When the moment is right, he strikes!

The deer's brays at the limit of its vocal cords. The sound echoes through the woods.

EXT. ANDOVER WOODS - SMALL CAVE - LATER

LIAM is revealed as the hooded man; covered in blood in the area near his mouth.

The deer's remains are sprawled out by the cave.

He looks at an old handkerchief in his dirty hands.

He throws it to the side and stares at his feet, trying to sit still and remember a time he almost forgot.

He ignores the existence of the handkerchief like it's an entity trying to whisper in his ear.

He hums to himself a song he used to hear every night; it's a faint memory from lifetimes ago.

He hums as if it'll block out the voices from the handkerchief.

INT. COTTAGE - IRELAND - NIGHT

The year is 1709 and a woman sings the same tune that Liam just was in the present.

She's his WIFE, and she holds an INFANT BABY in her arms. A prominent ring on her finger.

                    LIAM
                   (o.s.)
              It's the anniversa-
              ry of our wedding, you
              know.

She acknowledges him with a smile.

                    LIAM
                   (o.s.)
              And you know, a cer-
              tain somebody still
              owes me wine for sav-
              ing him last winter.

His charm suggests an idea.

She laughs with a breath, trying not to wake
the baby.

                    WIFE
              We can't possibly have
              a fifth child, Liam.

She tantalizes him. A look that suggests "We
shouldn't; but I want you to make it happen
anyway".

He laughs.

                    LIAM
                   (o.s.)
              Why not?

EXT. ANDOVER WOODS - SMALL CAVE - DAY

Liam has abandoned the cave. The handkerchief
has left with him, but the deer carcass remains.

TWO MEN look on at the cave and wonder aloud to
one another.

                    MAN 1
              You think it was a
              bear?

                    MAN 2
              A pack of coyotes,
              maybe.

INT. OLIVIA'S HOUSE - KITCHEN - NIGHT

OLIVIA helps her mother (PATRICIA) do the dishes after popcorn and sodas.

Patricia tires to probe her daughter for her
thoughts.

                    PATRICIA
              Good movie!

Olivia can't get the attack out of her mind.
She reaches for another dish and her mother
kisses her on the head.

                    PATRICIA
              I'm glad we watched
              it.

Olivia feigns a smile.

                    OLIVIA
              Me too.

Patricia scans her daughter, sensing something
is wrong.

                    PATRICIA
              Is everything okay?

Olivia struggles to seem fine.

                    OLIVIA
              Yeah!

                    PATRICIA
              You're sure?

                    OLIVIA
              Yeah, I'm just think-
              ing about- if I wan-
              na play trumpet in the

                      32

concert this summer.

                    PATRICIA
          You'd knock their
          socks off, honey. You
          still wanna go ahead
          with piano lessons
          too?

                    OLIVIA
          Yeah. I just wonder if
          I wanna have one last
          go at trumpet for fun.

                    PATRICIA
          It's up to you what
          you wanna do.- Oh,
          that's Bart in the
          driveway. Let me get
          him.

INT. OLIVIA'S HOUSE - OFFICE - LATER

OLIVIA looks at her Facebook feed.

Everyone is asking for Kayli to come back. The
oboist with the locker. She couldn't disappear
unless someone took her by force.

Olivia's heart sinks into her stomach.

PATRICIA rushes into the room for some last
words.

                    PATRICIA
          Okay, I'm off to Mal-
          den for the night.
          Will you be alright on
          your own?

                    OLIVIA
          I'll be fine.

Her mother hugs her.

                    PATRICIA
          Okay honey. I love
          you. Your father will
          be here tomorrow. He's
          staying up the road at
          the inn.

                    OLIVIA
          Okay. Have fun, Mom.

                    PATRICIA
          I love you, baby.

She plants a kiss on Olivia's head.

                    OLIVIA
          I love you too. Tell
          Bart to drive safe.

Olivia's mom runs off down the stairs to go off
with Bart.

                    PATRICIA
                    (o.s.)
          Your momma is his pre-
          cious cargo!

Olivia smirks, then looks back at the screen.
Her feelings sink again.

She looks down at PIGEON in the corner.

                    OLIVIA
          You're sleeping in MY
          room tonight.

EXT. WOODLAND PATH - ANDOVER - DAY

The birds sing an encore to the concert of the
year. The sun hangs low in the sky and OLIVIA
walks through the woods.

Deep in the distance, eyes watch her every
move.

INT. MEMORIAL HALL LIBRARY - ANDOVER - LATER

OLIVIA locks through jazz CDs upstairs. Piano
tracks of many kinds.

She gets a text from Girl 3 that reads "I'm
leaving my house now. I'll see you in a bit."

Olivia closes her phone and puts one of the CDs
back.

JAKE CUNNINGHAM, her ex boyfriend, appears at
one end of the aisle, like he looks through
classical music on his own time between contact
sports.

                    JAKE
          Hey. Can I talk with
          you for a second?

She doesn't want to deal with him, and yet she
feels guilty for feeling that way.

                    OLIVIA
          - Why?

Jake moves closer to speak in private.

                    JAKE
          Look. I'm sorry for
          what I said. I thought
          you were up to some-
          thing when you gave up
          on playing trumpet. I
          thought you might've
          been seeing someone.

                    OLIVIA
          - I want you to know
          for your sake, that I
          didn't take a break
          from trumpet to start
          seeing some guy. Just
          because I wasn't at
          rehearsal, it didn't
          mean I was UP to some-
          thing.

                    JAKE
Well I'm sorry. Just,
people are disappear-
ing and I heard it's
some new thing. It's
a lot of stoners from
what I hear.

                    OLIVIA
Jake, you of all peo-
ple should know I
don't smoke.

                    JAKE
Well some people knew
you gave up trumpet
and started talking.

                    OLIVIA
Golly. Thanks, Jake.
Now I know THAT's been
going on.

                    JAKE
Well if you j-

                    OLIVIA
I didn't "give up"
on trumpet, Jake. If
you heard me the first
time, you'd know why
I'm not playing at
school anymore.

                    JAKE
Well what is it?

                    OLIVIA
I just picked up an-
other instrument.

                    JAKE
What instrument?

                    OLIVIA
I don't care to tell

you.

                    JAKE
Why?

                    OLIVIA
Because I don't. I've
been avoiding you be-
cause I knew you'd try
to make things bet-
ter, but we just don't
match-!

A LIBRARIAN shushes her from behind.

She looks back at Jake and sees that he's
crushed; and she feels bad.

                    OLIVIA
                 (hushed)
We don't WORK togeth-
er. You want someone
more simple than me.
I'm obnoxious and com-
plicated!

                    JAKE
No you're-

                    OLIVIA
Jake, listen! You're
a nice guy. I think
you're great but
you're wasting your
time with me. I'm not
the one!

                    JAKE
Is it something I did?

                    OLIVIA
No Jake. It's us.
We're not compatible.
You want a different
life from me. The oth-
er day you said "If

we have kids" and the more I thought about it, we just don't match. You're so well put together that it scares me. I can't live a small town life. I can't just pop out two kids and get wrinkly without some adventure in my life, and there's no room for that in YOUR world. I can't be what you need. It's not in the cards for me. We're different people. Let's be adults and call it quits.

                    JAKE
But we're NOT adults.

                    OLIVIA
Jake.-

                    JAKE
You're wrong. And I'll PROVE you wrong.

                    OLIVIA
What the hell are you going to do? Mow a lawn better than anyone else? Jake, I wanna play a jazz club in Paris. Do you see yourself living in Paris?

Jake is at a loss for words. She's cold and it stings.

After a moment, he decides to sting her right back.

                    JAKE
          - You know, you'll
          always remember last
          summer no matter where
          you are.

This strikes a chord for her. Three months of
adventure and magic; when she hadn't realized
everything she knows now.

                    OLIVIA
          The best summer of my
          life so far; and I'll
          never forget it.

Her final composure states that she won't budge.
They're really, truly over.

Jake doesn't know what to do. His heart races.
He gives a huff to fight his tears as he walks
away. The burn of his words smolder behind him
in Olivia's heart.

EXT. JAKES BACK YARD - LATER

JAKE ties his shoes while his mom (MRS. CUN-
NINGHAM) opens the door.

                    MRS. CUNNINGHAM
          Jake, honey; I'm al-
          most done with dinner.

                    JAKE
          I know. I just need to
          go for a run.

                    MRS. CUNNINGHAM
          Are you okay?

                    JAKE
          Yeah. I just need to
          run.

                    MRS. CUNNINGHAM
          Okay. Just don't take
          long.

He steps onto a woodland path at the side of his property and starts jogging down the trail.

EXT. LAKESIDE - LATER

JAKE comes across a trash barrel and pulls photos out of his pocket. They're of him and Olivia.

He looks at them one last time, tears them apart and throws the photos into the barrel. He starts walking, taking his time; and that's when he hears it. A sound in the distance.

Approaching the sound, he comes to the untouched part of the woods. He listens close and hears it's the sound of a baby crying.

The crying becomes a scream! He breaks into a sprint!

All he can think about is an innocent child in danger. It's wailing. Rasping. Gurgling. Moaning.

He rounds a corner then falls in a hole!

He tumbles deep into the ground. He has no idea where he is. He looks up in a daze and sees a speaker. A shadow grows from the top of the hole.

EXT. TOWN PARK - BENCH - DAY

OLIVIA sits, waiting for her friend. LIAM looks on from the woods.

She has skull candy headphones and an I Pod Shuffle in her hoodie.

                    LIAM
          What's your good name,
          miss?

Olivia looks up at Liam. She takes a moment to gather what he's said. He spoke American En-

40

glish, but his choice of words was unusual.

                    OLIVIA
          I'm sorry?

                    LIAM
          What do they call you?

One headphone in her hand, she collects herself
and pretends it's normal.

                    OLIVIA
          My name is Olivia.

                    LIAM
          A pleasure.

She looks him over. A cleaned up version of
what he was. His clothing hangs in odd places,
almost like he stole them.

                    OLIVIA
          Where are you from?

                    LIAM
          I'm from Ireland.

Olivia feels at ease, assuming she's put it together. She finds it kinda funny; a good story
to tell her friend later.

                    LIAM
          Are you Irish?

                    OLIVIA
          Almost everybody is
          in this area; so I
          wouldn't doubt it.

                    LIAM
          You don't know your
          family's lineage?

                    OLIVIA
          I- Well I don't know
          my family tree. After

41

my great-grandma, your
guess is as good as
mine.

Liam takes the seat next to her.

                    LIAM
          I see. And what did
          SHE look like?

                    OLIVIA
          She's black, like me.

                    LIAM
          Mm. Persecution mud-
          dies the waters of
          history.- No doubt
          you've heard of what
          happened to the Irish.

                    OLIVIA
          I know a bit.

Liam offers his hand for her headphone.

                    LIAM
          May I?

Olivia hands him her headphone. He places it in
his ear like an ape experiencing technology for
the first time. He nods his head as he listens.

                    LIAM
          You have a musical
          talent, don't you?

                    OLIVIA
          I play the trumpet-
          but I'm taking up pi-
          ano.

                    LIAM
          A beautiful instru-
          ment. I would love to
          hear you play it.

                    OLIVIA
          Did you just move into
          town?

Liam is thrown off of his goal, but nods to answer before she grows suspicious.

                    OLIVIA
          Well, maybe I'll play
          for you sometime. Do
          you live far from
          here?

                    LIAM
          Just up the road.

                    OLIVIA
          Oh. I live in that di-
          rection!

                    LIAM
          Oh really!

                    OLIVIA
          What street do you
          live on?

Liam almost panics, but plays it cool. An aver-
age name should work.

                    LIAM
          - Main Street.

Olivia feels uneasy again. Her finger rises in
the opposite direction of where Liam has just
pointed.

                    OLIVIA
          Main Street is that
          way.-

Liam pretends his surprise.

                    LIAM
          Oh- I'm not really
          sure where it is. I

mean, just moved here.
I get turned around
all the time.

Olivia considers this could be true.

                    OLIVIA
          It's okay.

                    LIAM
          So, do you sing?

                    OLIVIA
          Not really.

                    LIAM
          Mm. How about I sing
          over your piano some-
          time.

Olivia decides he's harmless; maybe a good
friend in the making.

                    OLIVIA
          We can make a band.

Liam smiles for show, but his mind is elsewhere.

                    LIAM
          Yes. Let's do that.

                    OLIVIA
          We'll make it a plan,
          then. Come over any-
          time; I'll let you
          know when I'm ready
          and we can get start-
          ed.

Liam has hit success with what he wanted her to
say.

(GIRL 3) arrives and Liam becomes hurried to
leave.

                    GIRL 3
          Who is your friend,
          Olivia?

                    LIAM
          I'm Liam.

He can smell blood in the air, but he remains
polite. He puts out his hand for a handshake.

                    OLIVIA
          He's from Ireland.

                    LIAM
          If you'll excuse me,
          Olivia. There's some-
          thing I must attend to
          immediately.

                    OLIVIA
          Of course! Take care
          Liam!

Girl 3 gives Olivia a look that begs for details on the foreign man.

                    GIRL 3
          Where'd you meet him?

                    OLIVIA
          He just walked up to
          me!

                    GIRL 3
          He's SO European.-
          "Something I must at-
          tend to immediately".

                    OLIVIA
          I don't think that's
          usual for Irish peo-
          ple.

                    GIRL 3
          Well I like it, what-
          ever it is. He sounds

                       45

like a gentleman.

Olivia smirks as her friend takes her seat.

> GIRL 3
> What had you so up
> tight on the phone? It
> sounded serious. Was
> it Cunningham?

> OLIVIA
> No, but I did see him
> earlier.- That's an-
> other story for anoth-
> er time.-

> GIRL 3
> - Well, what is it?

Olivia chooses her words so her friend won't be
alarmed.

> OLIVIA
> This guy the other
> day- he ran up to me.
> He- sniffed me- and
> then left.

Girl 3's jaw drops.

> GIRL 3
> Oh my god! Back this
> up. What? Who?

Girl 3 can't help but laugh.

> OLIVIA
> A homeless guy behind
> Market Basket, where I
> work!

> GIRL 3
> Did you tell someone?

> OLIVIA
> No! My- my mom is off

on a vacation you see.
It's her honeymoon.
I'm home alone for a
week and I didn't wan-
na ruin her vacation.

                GIRL 3
Well are you alright?
You seem shaken up
about it.

                OLIVIA
It's those disappear-
ances.- When he came
up to me, he grabbed
my neck and it felt
like- like he was gon-
na kill me. You don't
think-.

                GIRL 3
I think it's worth
going to the police,
but if he was going to
kill you, I think he
would have done it.

                OLIVIA
I know but- if I tell
someone, then they'll
tell my Mom. I feel
like I should wait a
week.- I just don't
know. If it's some
killer, then I could
have evidence.

                GIRL 3
Look. The disappear-
ances are nothing for
you to worry about.
It's the druggies
leaving town to be
homeless in the city.
I heard Justine start-
ed doing heroin.

Olivia feels a pit in her stomach and Girl 3 nods.

                    GIRL 3
          You're worrying about
          nothing. Trust me. The
          real problem is much
          bigger than us.

Olivia sighs.

                    OLIVIA
          So it's not some kill-
          er.

Girl 3 grins.

                    GIRL 3
          Just a homeless guy
          with an odor fetish.

Olivia breathes out her relief in a laugh.

EXT. BACK WOODS TRAIN BRIDGE - NEW ENGLAND TOWN
- SUNSET

TWO MIDDLE SCHOOL BOYS use cans of deodorant
with a lighter to make blow-torches. They're
high on their laughter and a diet of candy.

Boy 2 reveals a firecracker he stole from his
brother's bedroom. He lights it and throws it
at Boy 1's feet.

It pops. A little scared, Boy 1 laugh.

                    BOY 1
          Idiot!

                    BOY 2
          Oh, dude!

Boy 2 points to the mouth of a sewer-tunnel.
There, a stream runs in.

He walks to the tunnel, lights a firecracker,

and throws it in.

                    BOY 1
          Y'know? This tunnel
          looks and smells a lot
          like your Mom's-

BANG!

The sound reverberates and shoots their jaws to
the floor in shock.

                    BOY 1
          Woah!

Boy 2 stands still.

He could swear he saw something in the flash of
the firecracker's light. It looked like a head-
less body sprawled like an adhesive at the bottom of the tunnel wall.

He steps back and his heel squishes something
off a solid surface. He's just peeled the flesh
off of a human head!

He screams!

Whoever did this could be near! They need help!

Boy 1 sees it too. The teeth on the bottom jaw
demand to be seen, sticking out of the soil;
white in the waning daylight.

INT. OLIVIA'S HOUSE - OLIVIA'S ROOM - NIGHT

OLIVIA lays in bed with a book. Its too shallow
and self-centered for her taste.

She closes the book and places it on the nightstand next to a photo of her and her father.

She looks at PIGEON. He lays in his dog bed.

                    OLIVIA
          That's the last time I

take a book recommen-
dation from Becky.

Pigeon tilts his head, trying to read her face.

Olivia looks at another photo on her nightstand
right by the open window.

It's a music recital. Kayli is among the group.

Olivia looks at Pigeon, pondering.

                    OLIVIA
          Kayli wouldn't run
          away.-

Pigeon doesn't understand but looks at her.

Olivia's phone buzzes.

She clicks it open.

                    MRS. CUNNINGHAM
          Olivia, when did you
          see Jake today?

                    OLIVIA
          Mrs. Cunningham? How
          did you know I saw
          Jake?

                    MRS. CUNNINGHAM
          Please Olivia. Becky
          said you saw him ear-
          lier!

                    OLIVIA
          He was at the library.
          It was maybe three
          o'clock. He's not
          home?

                    MRS. CUNNINGHAM
          He came home but he
          disappeared! You saw
          each other before he

came home?

                    OLIVIA
          Yes Mrs. Cunningham, I
          haven't seen him since
          we ran into each other
          at the library.

               MRS. CUNNINGHAM
          He's not at your
          house? Is your mother
          home?

                    OLIVIA
          Mrs. Cunningham, my
          mom is on her honey-
          moon. I'm supposed to
          see my dad tomorrow. I
          wouldn't lie to you.

               MRS. CUNNINGHAM
          Okay;- if you hear
          anything, let me know.
          And be careful!

                    OLIVIA
          I will, Mrs. Cunning-
          ham.

Mrs. Cunningham hangs up. Olivia drops her
phone on the bed. She stands up to think.

There's a knock! It's the front door.

INT. OLIVIA'S HOUSE - FRONT DOOR - CONTINUOUS

OLIVIA looks from afar to see who's there. It's
LIAM on the other side. She approaches and
opens it a crack.

                    OLIVIA
          Hi uh- Liam? What are
          you doing here?

                    LIAM
          You said I could come

over anytime. I figured
now was as good a time
as any.

                    OLIVIA
          By "anytime" I didn't
          mean unannounced.

                    LIAM
          Yes. Forgive my rude-
          ness, but there's
          something important I
          need to tell you.

                    OLIVIA
          Well, let's hear it.

                    LIAM
          Could you open your
          door a little?

Olivia opens the door. She hopes he won't call
her bluff.

                    OLIVIA
          I'll have you know,
          Pigeon is more fero-
          cious than he looks.

PIGEON cowers behind her.

                    OLIVIA
          My mother is waiting
          upstairs for me too,
          so make it quick.

Liam thinks it would be nice to put her in her
place for assuming the worst of him.

Olivia's cellphone buzzes upstairs.

                    LIAM
          I came here to extend
          an apology.

52

                    OLIVIA
          You have nothing to be
          sorry about.

                    LIAM
          But I do.

                    OLIVIA
          You took a shot and
          introduced yourself.
          Now you're being a
          creep on my doorstep.

                    LIAM
          Well; you have all the
          answers now, don't
          you?

Olivia is taken aback.

                    LIAM
          I promise you, that
          you have nothing to
          fear. You might be
          surprised but I don't
          have so much as an
          ounce of malicious in-
          tent.

Olivia wants him to get to the point. She can't
figure out if she should be sorry or afraid.

                    OLIVIA
          I don't follow.

The home phone rings.

                    LIAM
          I didn't meet you in
          the park by coinci-
          dence. I introduced
          myself with a pur-
          pose.- I need to know
          who you are. You see,
          I've seen you once be-
          fore. In the back of

the market where you
work.

Olivia's stomach drops.

                    OLIVIA
          What?

The answering machine plays.

                    GIRL 3
          (o.s.)
          Olivia! Call me back
          when you can! A boy
          found a body in the
          river by town hall.
          Please call me!

Olivia looks into the eyes of a killer and he
glares right back.

                    LIAM
          I'd like to see you
          try and run.

Olivia SLAMS the door!

She runs for the phone. The power is off!

Breaking and crashing in the basement!

She runs for her cell phone! Up the stairs!

Clawing! Pounding footsteps on the side of the
house!

INT. OLIVIA'S HOUSE - OLIVIA'S ROOM - CONTINU-
OUS

OLIVIA catches herself! She's leaning on the
doorway.

LIAM is already there, holding her cellphone.

Olivia turns! Liam grabs her! His hand, over
her mouth!

                    LIAM
          I would never hurt you
          Olivia. You are the
          first person I've spo-
          ken to in a long time!
          You're my own flesh and
          blood! I cannot harm
          you.

Olivia lets up on her fighting. She fails to
squirm away; to make a comment, to ask a question or yell for help.

She's at his mercy.

                    LIAM
          Olivia, I don't want
          to scare you. It's not
          my intention.-

He has a second thought on this.

                    LIAM
          Well, maybe a lit-
          tle after you were so
          rude.- But I'm not
          about to harm my own
          family.- That's what
          I am. I'm your fami-
          ly. Your ancestor; and
          I so desperately need
          you to hear my story.
          Now. Not later.

He feels like a monster, holding her mouth shut
like this.

                    LIAM
          I'm so sorry. Please,
          will you listen? I
          promise, after I've
          told you everything,
          I'll leave immediate-
          ly.

Olivia decides she's willing to hear him. He

takes his hand off her mouth and she doesn't scream. She listens.

                    LIAM
          It was three-hun-
          dred years ago. I had
          my wife and our four
          children. Twin boys,
          John and Ian. They
          were the oldest. The
          youngest was an in-
          fant, Paul. Lastly,
          between them, there
          was my only daugh-
          ter, Lilly.- I sold my
          crops to a business
          partner. He owned a
          pub in a port-town by
          the sea.- After sav-
          ing him one winter,
          he owed me.- He kept
          his end of the bargain
          and held the bottle of
          wine aside for me.- On
          the night of my anni-
          versary with my wife,
          we decided to cele-
          brate. I went and saw
          my friend that night.
          I remember he said
          something wasn't right
          about the night.- I
          went against his ad-
          vice and made for home
          with the bottle.- On
          the way back there was
          this child. She looked
          like she was Lil-
          ly's age. She looked
          scared, and I asked if
          she was okay.- There
          was something twist-
          ed- demonic about her
          face. She bit me,- and
          so did her friends.- I
          made my way out of it

56

by putting some dis-
tance between us.- I
made for home, but
somewhere along the
way, I fell. I woke,
feeling- a headache.-
and I burned all
over as the sky grew
brighter.- Made it up
the hill, to my home,-
and-.

INT. LIAM'S COTTAGE - FRONT DOOR - MORNING 1712

LIAM SLAMS the door open. He's hyperventilat-
ing. He looks around. It's a mess.

He makes his way up the stairs. There's hints
of a struggle. One of his sons is dead on the
floor in a doorway.

He screams but continues for the others.

Liam looks into the other rooms.

There's nothing.

Nothing.

Finally, where he and his wife would sleep,
there he sees what's left of his wife and sons.

His vision blurs in madness as he screams.

INT. OLIVIA'S HOUSE - OLIVIA'S ROOM - CONTINU-
OUS

LIAM can't find the words.

OLIVIA looks at him; unable to believe what
he's told her, but then again, it explains how
he scaled the side of the house.

INT. LIAM'S COTTAGE - BEDROOM - MORNING 1712

LIAM places all the remains in the bed. He

tucks them in to keep them together.

His wife's ring is missing from her finger, and he gathers his brows.

His stomach churns with pain. He falls on his knees.

                    LIAM
                   (v.o.)
          I began to feel sick.

He looks at a dark red-brown spot on the wooden floor. He can smell it from here.

He hits the floor and drags his tongue over the grit and dirt on the spot, savoring the iron-tasting hint within it.

                    LIAM
               The only thing that
               made it better, was
               blood.

INT. OLIVIA'S HOUSE - OLIVIA'S ROOM - CONTINU-OUS

LIAM collects himself. His wandering mind is realigned.

                    LIAM
               The only one miss-
               ing, was Lilly. I nev-
               er found her body.
               -For years and years
               I looked, and I
               thought she might have
               died that day; but I
               couldn't just accept
               it without proof.- I
               would have given up
               if I knew she was
               dead; but nothing for
               three-hundred years.-
               Nothing until the oth-
               er day. I had no de-

sire for your blood.
It just wasn't there.
You smelled different.
I couldn't figure out
what it was until I
realized, you were de-
scended from me. -That
could only happen if
you were descended
from my lost child, my
daughter.

OLIVIA looks long at him. He has large cuts on
him, but no blood. His body looks dead.

                    OLIVIA
          If that's true, then
          what am I supposed to
          do about anything?
          I'm in high school.
          -You're telling me
          you're a vampire. Do
          you have any idea how
          crazy I'd look helping
          you?

                    LIAM
          You don't need to do
          much of anything at
          all. I wear sunblock
          during the day; I can
          investigate things my-
          self.

                    OLIVIA
          What happens if you're
          exposed to the sun?

                    LIAM
          You really wouldn't
          like to see it.

                    OLIVIA
          - How do you eat?

                    59

                    LIAM
I'm on a more- re-
stricted diet.

                    OLIVIA
Did you kill the per-
son they found today?

                    LIAM
Yes, that was me.

                    OLIVIA
H- how is that "re-
stricted"?!

                    LIAM
He was selling chil-
dren. The man they
found was someone my
previous target would
buy- children from.

                    OLIVIA
Did you save a child
from him?

                    LIAM
Yes, and every child
he won't take from
this point onward.

                    OLIVIA
What about Kayli, Jake
and the others? What
did they do?

                    LIAM
You're asking about
the missing people?

                    OLIVIA
Do you know where they
are?

                    LIAM
That's what brought me

to this town in the
first place.

                OLIVIA
        You're some sort of
        hero or something?

                LIAM
        I follow the signs of
        vampire infestations.
        In case my daughter is
        like me.

                OLIVIA
        And if you find her,
        are you gonna start
        killing people togeth-
        er?

                LIAM
        I'll move to animal
        blood. That way I can
        age and die, like nor-
        mal.

                OLIVIA
        - And what if you
        don't find her?

Liam is silent.

                LIAM
        I hope to find proof
        that she died peace-
        fully as a human be-
        ing; not like what I
        am now. -Although self-
        ishly; seeing her again
        wouldn't be the worst
        of fates.

                OLIVIA
        I don't know what you
        want me to do. I can
        barely drive.

                        61

                    LIAM
          What about your par-
          ents?

                    OLIVIA
          W-? My mom is out of
          town!
                    LIAM
          And your father?

                    OLIVIA
          I'm supposed to see
          him tomorrow, but I
          promise he's a lost
          cause.

Liam sees the photo of her with her father on
the nightstand by the open window.

                    LIAM
          Why-so?

                    OLIVIA
          Because he can bare-
          ly be bothered with
          me, Liam! I doubt
          he'll make time for a
          long lost relative!
          -Can you just please
          go? You've given me a
          heart attack and I'm
          really looking forward
          to a good night of
          sleep. You know, ever
          since you attacked me
          the other day I hav-
          en't been able to shut
          my eyes! Every second
          I've been fearing and
          reliving it, over and
          over in my head!

                    LIAM
          I'm sorry, Olivia; I
          truly am.

                    62

                    OLIVIA
          I- I just can't with
          this right now. Can
          you please go?

Liam opens his mouth but hesitates.

                    OLIVIA
          Don't you dare ask to
          stay here. You're not
          welcome!

                    LIAM
          No, I- I just want-
          ed to know where your
          father is staying to-
          night.

She bites her teeth together, reluctant to
tell.

                    LIAM
          For my daughter, Oliv-
          ia. Please.

                    OLIVIA
          He's staying at the
          Andover Inn, up the
          road. I doubt he'll be
          any help.

                    LIAM
          Thank you, Olivia.

He plants both his feet on the window frame.

                    OLIVIA
          And don't you dare
          hurt him!

Liam can't bear to look back at her, but tries
to. His face admits his remorse for his behav-
ior.

                    LIAM
          I wouldn't dream of

it.

He jumps out of the window without a sound, and Olivia breaths easier, knowing she isn't responsible for withholding information on her attacker.

She looks to her desk and notices the photo of her and her father is missing.

                    OLIVIA
          What an asshole!

EXT. BACK PATIO - THE ANDOVER INN - NIGHT

Olivia's father, LIONEL, is sitting at a patio table with a glass of whiskey. He notices a WOMAN with a slim-thick build and a tight dress.

She gives him a look. She's interested, and he smiles.

LIAM comes in from behind Lionel and sits in front of him to block his view of the woman. Liam holds a wine glass, but the wine looks thick and sticks to walls of the glass.

                    LIAM
          She's not your type.

                    LIONEL
          Where the-?

Lionel looks behind him, and there's nothing but wilderness and a pond.

                    LIONEL
          Just how long were you
          behind me?

Liam laughs.

                    LIAM
          Just came around the
          building from the oth-

er side; didn't mean
to scare ya.

Lionel is still creeped out; perhaps homopho-
bic.

                    LIONEL
          Who are you to say
          what I'd like?

                    LIAM
          She's been having
          a little more than
          drinks tonight.

Lionel can't figure out what he's getting at.
She seems relatively normal.

                    LIAM
          She likes her pills;
          perhaps a little TOO
          much.

                    LIONEL
          -Sounds like a night-
          mare.- Thanks for the
          heads up.

                    LIAM
          Don't mention it. Tell
          me your name.

Lionel is offended by his forwardness.

                    LIONEL
          I'm Lionel.

                    LIAM
          Liam.- It's a plea-
          sure.

Liam scoots his seat around the table to talk
more privately, and they shake hands.

Lionel can't decide if Liam is foreign or what,

but he talks funny.

> LIAM
> Tell me, you seem old
> enough to have a wife
> and children. Why
> would someone like you
> be on the prowl any-
> way?

Lionel starts thinking that Liam is INTENTION-
ALLY rude, but he choses to be polite either
way.

> LIONEL
> I was. I divorced. I'm
> actually in town to
> see my daughter.

> LIAM
> Oh, bless you then.
> I'm sorry to hear it.

Lionel can't imagine Liam is really that sorry
to hear about something so common.

> LIAM
> Are you excited to see
> her?

> LIONEL
> I- I am.

> LIAM
> I sense hesitance.

Liam digs into feelings that Lionel refuses to
discuss. It's a gnawing sensation but what does
it matter? He'll leave soon enough and Lionel
doesn't want to make a scene.

> LIONEL
> Yeah, well I can't
> seem to do the right
> thing no matter what I
> do.- You shower your

kid with everything
you never had and she
still has you come
to this God forsaken
place.- For what? I-
can't figure that out.

                LIAM
This town holds memo-
ries of your wife.-

                LIONEL
Ex wife.

                LIAM
Right.- Well it's
funny how that hap-
pens, isn't it? Our
kids never appreciate
what we wanted when WE
were children. We have
to listen for THEIR
needs, and not the
ones that WE had.

Lionel takes a second to digest what Liam just
said.

                LIONEL
Hold on. You have
kids?

                LIAM
Had them.

Lionel is halted in asking more. The implica-
tion of that correction makes his hair stand on
end.

                LIAM
Does that surprise
you?

                LIONEL
Sorry, you just- look
a little young.- You

see, I was living the
bachelor life until
twenty-eight. Hell,
if I wrapped it up, I
still wouldn't have a
kid!

Lionel laughs but the joke falls flat this time.
This isn't a matter of small talk.

                    LIAM
          I guess that's the
          luxury of living in a
          world where people get
          to grow old.

Lionel readjusts. It seems there are sensitive
subjects that this man has yet to reveal.

                    LIONEL
          Where are your kids
          now? Did your wife
          take 'em?- From what
          you said, I just fig-
          ure-.

                    LIAM
          - Three of them are
          dead. -One is missing.

Lionel is paralyzed.

                    LIAM
          I've had more than
          enough time to come to
          terms with the oth-
          er three.- What haunts
          me, with my daughter
          Lilly, is how changed
          she'll be if and when
          I find her.- All those
          lost years and I won-
          der what she even
          looks like anymore.- I
          don't mean to make it
          so you're unable to

enjoy your place in
the world, but- don't
neglect the time you
have with your daugh-
ter.- There's no price
I can pay to get mine
back.- All that time
is priceless.- Do your
family a service and
listen to what they
need from you. We are
fathers. We provide,
with every fiber of our
being; until we have
nothing left to give.

The slim-thick woman brays a yawn to get Lionel's attention. He looks her way, then ignores
it. He looks back to Liam, but he's gone.

The wine glass is still on the table.

                    WAITER
          Last call, sir. Will
          you be closing your
          tab?

Lionel looks to the WAITER.

                    LIONEL
          Uh- yes please.

The waiter asks for the glasses. He hands his
own, then reaches for Liam's. He notices a
dried stain on the inside of the glass. It
looks similar to a scab.

Lionel feels his face go numb. He looks to the
dark woods behind the inn. He sees and hears
nothing.

INT. TOOLSHED - LATER

LIAM stares at the photo of Olivia and Lionel,
trying to remember.

                    LIAM
              Maybe you look like
              her- I can't remember.

Before his inner eyes is a blurred shadow of
his wife's face. Just the aura she once had
when she was alive.
He looks at the handkerchief in his other hand.

EXT. LAKESIDE - TWO-HUNDRED YEARS AGO - EVENING

LIAM sees a woman bathing in the lake. He tries
to hide his eyes, but he can't help looking.

She's beautiful; but he walks away and waits
for her to dress.

When she's clothed, she wears a BLUE DRESS; and
that's when Liam approaches.

                    LIAM
              Hello.

                    BLUE DRESS
              Were you watching me?

                    LIAM
              No. I waited until you
              were clothed. I may
              have seen briefly but
              it wasn't intentional.
              I'm sorry.

                    BLUE DRESS
              Well what do you want?
              You're a stranger.

                    LIAM
              I was just traveling
              through and well, I
              don't talk to people
              often. I thought you
              might-.

                    BLUE DRESS
              Are you a gypsy?

> LIAM
> No, I'm- catholic from
> Ireland. I'm sorry, I
> just don't know if I'd
> be able to introduce
> myself again.

> BLUE DRESS
> You could've pretended
> you didn't see me- and
> try at a time when I
> haven't just bathed.

Liam looks at a loss for words.

> LIAM
> That would be dishon-
> est. I wouldn't dream
> of doing that.

She pulls out a shiny silky handkerchief. She
uses it to wipe hair oils off her hands. As she
does, she smirks at him.

INT. TOOLSHED - NIGHT 2011

LIAM looks at the same handkerchief in the mod-
ern day. It's next to the picture of Olivia,
which he lowers.

The handkerchief is dirty and ragged. It
doesn't shine. It's more brown than blue like
it was. The same as her dress.

> LIAM
> Please, let me forget
> you.

INT. CAFE NIRO - BOOTH SEAT - DAY

OLIVIA is seated with her text book and a notebook open. Behind her, two GIRLS mutter back
and forth.

> GIRL 4
> I heard Jake Cunning-

ham went missing last
night.

                    GIRL 5
          Do you think he killed
          that homeless guy?

                    GIRL 4
          What?!

They look at one another, half-serious, then
laugh.

                    GIRL 4
          No. Jake's harmless.

The girls look in Olivia's direction and whisper.

Olivia dreads the rumor they're concocting;
"but on the other hand," she thinks "in a little over a year this school will be long behind
me".

LIONEL jaunts up to her table with two hot apple ciders. He wears a smile, and it looks different from usual.

                    OLIVIA
          Dad, what th-?

                    LIONEL
          Come on, I know you
          love it.

He places the ciders down and kisses her head
in a hug.

The two girls watch him. They swoon over the
fatherly gestures.

Lionel takes his seat opposite Olivia. She
closes her books.

                    OLIVIA
          You're a coffee guy.

What's with the sudden
change?

                    LIONEL
          Can't a guy have a
          sweet tooth?

He protrudes his lips and sips his cider like
it's the queen of England's tea.

She laughs and holds her cup to feel its
warmth. It's too hot for her to have a sip yet.

                    OLIVIA
          This feels familiar.

                    LIONEL
          It does. Too bad
          there's no snow on the
          ground, though.- Do
          you have any ideas for
          the day?

She shakes her head.

                    LIONEL
          Well, I saw this fly-
          er on the board over
          there. I wanna know
          what you think.

He passes her the flyer and she looks it over.

She raises a brow.

                    OLIVIA
          Uh- No-.

She laughs. He can't possibly want to go there.

                    LIONEL
          Are you so sure?

                    OLIVIA
          Oh my God, I-. Uh-uh,
          I can't.

                    LIONEL
          You look pretty curi-
          ous!

Olivia sighs, smiling. He's right, but she's
also scared.
INT. HAUNTED HOUSE - SPOOKY WORLD - NIGHT

OLIVIA screams! Her father (LIONEL) laughs with
his hands on her shoulders.

He walks with her through the house of hor-
rors. The ACTORS in monster costumes scream and
threaten with fake weapons.

EXT. PICNIC TABLE - SPOOKY WORLD - LATER

OLIVIA eats fried dough with her father, LIO-
NEL.

                    LIONEL
          A pretty good idea,
          huh?

                    OLIVIA
          You certainly know
          how to make a night I
          can't forget.

                    LIONEL
          For better or worse.

They smile at one another. It's been too long
since they've had anything like this.

                    OLIVIA
          Why'd you wanna do
          this anyway? I thought
          you wanted to go off
          someplace fancy.

Lionel doesn't talk about emotions, and so he
drudges up the words as he says them.

                    LIONEL
          - My favorite thing in

the whole-wide world
is to see you smile.-
See, this guy, he told
me how he lost his
daughter and well- it
put some things in
perspective.

Olivia realizes it must have been Liam.

                    LIONEL
          My parents didn't have
          money.- I've always
          wanted to give you
          what I never had,- but
          that's not what YOU
          want. Money isn't what
          you're worried about.-
          You just want a little
          of my time.

Olivia fignts tears that she didn't even know
she had.

                    LIONEL
          We've got more haunted
          houses if you're done
          with that dough.

                    OLIVIA
          You're hell-bent on
          traumatizing me.

He rubs her head and cackles. He's proud that
she's inherited his humor.

EXT. WOODLAND PATH - ANDOVER - DAY

OLIVIA walks on her way to school. In the middle of the path LIAM waits for her.

She halts for a moment. It's an awkward re-
union.

                    OLIVIA
          You stole my picture

of me and my dad.

He breathes deep and opens his mouth, but he has nothing to say.

                    OLIVIA
          Just because you got
          my dad to listen to
          me, it doesn't make
          us good.- You still
          damaged my house and
          scared the shit out of
          me.

He reaches into his jacket pocket and reveals the photo he took. Olivia takes it from him.

                    LIAM
          I'm sorry I had to
          take this, and I'm
          sorry still for the
          other day.- I'll re-
          pair any damages.

                    OLIVIA
          Well then.- How are
          things? Did you find
          what you needed?

                    LIAM
          - I, uh-

                    OLIVIA
          What is it?

                    LIAM
          - Well I need to be
          quick. I apologize
          again, but the more
          time wasted, the cold-
          er the trail gets. I
          need to ask about Jake
          Cunningham, do you
          know him?

                    OLIVIA
          He's my ex boyfriend.

                    LIAM
          Really? He's your-?

                    OLIVIA
          Yes.

                    LIAM
          Okay- well I need some
          information from some-
          one close to him.

                    OLIVIA
          I could ask his cous-
          in.

Liam is in disbelief that she's offering to
help him. It's been so long since he could rely
on family. He almost forgot what it felt like.

                    OLIVIA
          You really didn't kill
          him?

                    LIAM
          No.- No, I've been on
          animal blood. Ever
          since I met you.

                    OLIVIA
          - If you don't mind me
          asking, why did you go
          after me behind the
          grocery store? If you
          don't kill innocent
          people then why did
          you attack me?

                    LIAM
          I- haven't spoken to
          anyone in a long time.
          -I don't know how to
          behave anymore. -I'm
          sorry.

Olivia sighs without anything further to say.

                    LIAM
          - Look, if you're
          willing to ask some
          questions for me,
          then I'd need you to
          ask them exactly as I
          say them.- Again, the
          trail is going cold.

Olivia nods, ready to listen.

INT. ANDOVER HIGH SCHOOL - HALLWAY - LATER

OLIVIA consoles Jake's COUSIN with her tone as
she asks.

                    OLIVIA
          What did they hear
          from him last? Where
          was he going?

The cousin isn't in tears, but she's sick to
her stomach with nerves; and it has her thinking of crying very often.

                    COUSIN
          He went on a run. I
          don't know the route
          he'd take, but he'd
          start on the path be-
          hind his house.

                    OLIVIA
          Was that usual for him
          to do that? I mean, at
          that time of day?

                    COUSIN
          Yeah; sometimes he'd
          only be gone a lit-
          tle while, but there's
          been times that he'd
          take a little longer
          than usual. That's why

his mom didn't think
anything about it at
first.

Olivia knows he'd either be seeing her or someone else, and that's the reason why he'd be
late sometimes.

She can't help but sound sarcastic.

                    OLIVIA
          I know.

The cousin is confused. Olivia struggles to re-
cover.

                    OLIVIA
          Was he seeing someone?

                    COUSIN
          Oh, no. He was heart-
          broken about you.

Olivia stifles the feeling this gives her. Her
face feels flush with flattery, but her stomach
churns with guilt; but that's not what matters
right now.

She just wants the answers that Liam needs.
It's her best chance of saving Jake if he's
still alive.

                    OLIVIA
          That's not my concern.
          I just need to know
          where he was at the
          time he went missing.

EXT. ENTRANCE TO WOODLAND PATH - ANDOVER - LAT-
ER

OLIVIA steps out of her car while LIAM steps
off of the path. They both start looking around
the area for clues.

                    LIAM
          Are you sure this is
          the path?

Liam squats and scans the ground with his eyes.

                    OLIVIA
          It was the one he'd
          take a month ago.

                    LIAM
          Right- well; I don't
          smell a drop of blood.

                    OLIVIA
          That's why time was so
          important.-

Liam stands and scrunches his brows.

                    LIAM
          Do you know of any
          abandoned buildings in
          the area?

                    OLIVIA
          Why? Did you find some-
          thing?

                    LIAM
          No, just something I'd
          like to check. -After
          tracking vampires for
          three-hundred years,
          you learn their hab-
          its.

                    OLIVIA
          I don't like where
          this is going.-

Liam doesn't respond but hurries into her car,
seating himself in the passenger's side.

I/E. OLIVIA'S CAR - ENTRANCE TO WOODLAND PATH -
CONTINUOUS

OLIVIA opens the car door. LIAM looks her way
after noticing that she hasn't seated herself.

                    OLIVIA
              Can you get in the
              trunk, please?

                    LIAM
              What? Why?

                    OLIVIA
              I'm on my J.O.L.

                    LIAM
              Pardon?

                    OLIVIA
              My Junior Operating
              License. There's some
              people that I can't
              have in the car while
              I drive; and you're
              one of them.

Liam doesn't protest, but gets out of the car
and goes to the trunk.

I/E. OLIVIA'S CAR - OLIVIA'S HOUSE DRIVEWAY -
LATER

OLIVIA puts the car in park and slides through
the gap to the back seat.

She speaks through the back of the seat to
LIAM.

                    OLIVIA
              Hey, the sky cleared
              up and the sun is out.
              Do you want to stay
              here until the sun
              goes down?

                    LIAM
              Just open the back
              seat. There should be

a latch somewhere.

Olivia pulls the latch and the back seat falls open. Liam peers out from the darkness. He crawls out to join her and closes the seat behind him.

> OLIVIA
> Why'd you come out
> like that?-

She looks at the sunlight outside.

> OLIVIA
> You seem fine to me.-

> LIAM
> My condition with the
> sun is better behind
> glass; especially car
> windows.

> OLIVIA
> It must be ultraviolet
> light.

She reaches into the center console and grabs sunblock to throw at Liam. He catches it and looks long at it.

He knows the term "sunblock" but "ultraviolet" is something he's never heard aloud, let alone understood when he's read the term on a bottle.

> LIAM
> Yes- it must be that.

He's aware that he seems out of the loop, but he doesn't care. He applies the sunblock as he talks.

> LIAM
> It's your mother's
> side, by the way.

OLIVIA
Huh?

LIAM
Your father is not re-
lated to me.
OLIVIA
- If you knew that,
then why'd you tell
him about your missing
daughter?

LIAM
Well, -someone had
to put his head on
straight.

OLIVIA
- You said before that
you hunt vampires be-
cause you think your
daughter might be one.

LIAM
Lilly is my daughter's
name; and yes.

OLIVIA
What do you do when
they're not Lilly?

LIAM
If they're a vampire,
I leave them alone,
and that's only hap-
pened a handful of
times.- Finding vam-
pires and killing
them are two differ-
ent things. Even if I
win, there's a chance
they'll seriously in-
jure me.- But; if it's
a serial killer, then
I do the community a
favor.

83

                    OLIVIA
          You really didn't kill
          any of the missing
          people in town?

                    LIAM
          Other than the crimi-
          nal, no. Like I said,
          I stay away from the
          innocent.

                    OLIVIA
          You should see his
          picture on the news.

                    LIAM
          A picture of the man I
          killed?

                    OLIVIA
          Yeah. His high school
          yearbook photo.

                    LIAM
          Well- he was someone's
          child once too.-

                    OLIVIA
          Yeah, but he was a
          horrible person, so
          it's whatever.

                    LIAM
          - Yeah. -Right.

He's remorseful and doesn't know how to break
it to her.

Olivia looks long at him. He's been suffering.

                    OLIVIA
          Come in the house.
          I'll help you find
          those abandoned build-
          ings.

INT. OLIVIA'S HOUSE - OFFICE - LATER

OLIVIA shows LIAM the town of Andover on Google Maps.

                    OLIVIA
          These are all the
          abandoned buildings
          in town. Down by the
          tracks, Lower Shaw-
          sheen, and way out
          this way, by River
          Road.

                    LIAM
          The only one that
          makes sense to me is
          Lower Shawsheen. If
          there was any place,
          that's where they'd
          go.

                    OLIVIA
          Why there?

                    LIAM
          All the traffic. Nobody
          notices a disappear-
          ance in a place where
          someone can make-off
          in any direction.- All
          these intersections,
          the highway; that and
          there's no churches.

                    OLIVIA
          Why churches?

                    LIAM
          They're more likely to
          notice when you're in
          town. They're willing
          to believe in vampires
          so they put the pieces
          together faster than
          anyone else.

EXT. ABANDONED BUILDING - LOWER SHAWSHEEN - SUNSET

OLIVIA pulls into the driveway and steps out to open the trunk.

LIAM crawls out to look over the building. The paint on the window frames is cracked and curled. Weeds reach out of cracks in the pavement that leads to a loading dock.

Olivia knows it's a matter of time until the vampire can come out of the building.

                    OLIVIA
          The sun is going
          down.-

                    LIAM
          There's enough time.
          You'll be fine, just
          stay in the car. Don't
          open the door, and
          keep the windows up,
          no matter what.

Olivia steps into the car and locks the door. She locks her eyes onto Liam's every move as he walks toward the building.

INT. ABANDONED BUILDING - LOWER SHAWSHEEN - CONTINUOUS

A large room like a garage covered in "666", pentagrams, and satanic symbols. There is a nutcracker in the middle of the floor. Its face is sanded off.

Through a doorway, LIAM submerges into the darkness of the following room.

The plaster has left the walls from years of erosion; leaving wood bare to the black-mold laden air.

A vat in the corner of the room contains the

acid-dissolving remains of a used body. Three other bodies hang upside down from the ankle, wrapped in chains that hang from a support beam. Underneath each one is a bucket.

Their blood drips from cuts on their bodies. It collects into the buckets like some ritual.

                    LIAM
          Dear God.-

                    ARCTURUS
          All my years,- I nev-
          er guessed I would see
          you again.

Liam looks to ARCTURUS, a withering vampire of Roman origin. He was powerful once. A self-indulging glutton of refined tastes. Now he's a shadow of his former self.

                    LIAM
          Arcturus?

                    ARCTURUS
          I'm surprised you re-
          member my name.

                    LIAM
          You look horrible.

                    ARCTURUS
          Yes. An accident
          left me buried in a
          coal mine for a long
          while.- I starved, and
          so I lost my luster.
          I've tried- and I'm
          still trying to find
          some way to reverse
          the effects. I've been
          targeting the youth
          for that purpose;
          though my findings are
          inconclusive.

He gestures toward the hanging bodies. The GUY who was smoking (dead), KAYLI (seemingly dead), and JAKE (alive).

> ARCTURUS
> - I tried to feed on infants for a while, but it bore no fruit. It's my hope that- over time, the youth may- suffice.- Besides, they're easier when they're older- out on their own.

Liam hides his disgust.

> LIAM
> You still marinate your blood, I see.

Arcturus laughs.

> ARCTURUS
> Yes, although; I've had to change to a trapping strategy, on account of my condition.

He gestures to a speaker he has.

> ARCTURUS
> Have you found another vampire maiden? If I remember correctly, you and Dahlia were a pair when I met you. You were feeding on animal blood.

> LIAM
> Have you seen Dahlia?

> ARCTURUS
> You did not hear?

Liam shakes his head.

> ARCTURUS
> Dahlia went clean. She
> passed on.
>> LIAM
>> She did?

> ARCTURUS
> She grew old without
> you.

Liam nods.

> LIAM
> Good. I'm glad of it.

> ARCTURUS
> Why did you want to
> be immortal? I don't
> remember. You didn't
> seem the type for it.

> LIAM
> It was to find my
> daughter.

> ARCTURUS
> That's right! Dahl-
> ia went with me for a
> stint after you left.-
> It was because of you
> that she left the path
> of aging for a while.

Arcturus laughs, thinking the righteous path is
weakness. Liam feels a need to defend her and
can't help but speak against Arcturus' glutton-
ous ways.

> LIAM
> Well, I'm glad she
> found it again.

> ARCTURUS
> - Tell me, have you

had any luck?

                    LIAM
          Actually, I found a
          descendant of mine in
          this town. A girl.

                    ARCTURUS
          So your daughter lived
          and died, then?

                    LIAM
          I don't know.

                    ARCTURUS
          You think vampire
          blood flows through
          this descendant's
          veins?

                    LIAM
               I-

He looks at Arcturus. His face is beckoning. He
thinks Olivia's blood is the key to his regen-
eration.

                    LIAM
          No. No we can't breed.

                    ARCTURUS
          You know this?

                    LIAM
          I've tried.

Arcturus hisses and stomps! He whips his de-
meanor back to that of a gentleman. He struggles to maintain the illusion as he tries to
negotiate.

                    ARCTURUS
          What of a drop?

                    LIAM
               No.

                    ARCTURUS
          A vile of her elixir!

                     LIAM
          No!

                    ARCTURUS
          What if a woman can
          bear-!

                     LIAM
          I said no!

They look at one another. They already know
where this is going. Their minds have been set.

They collide!

They rip!

They tear!

Fists pound!

They roar like grizzlies!

The rumble of the room, like a hurricane,
churning round and round!

Arcturus has the upper hand with a stake at Liam's heart!

Liam throws the stake aside!

He sees sunlight!

Just a crack through the unstable wall!

He launches Arcturus through the wall and into
the sunlight!

EXT. ABANDONED BUILDING - LOWER SHAWSHEEN -
CONTINUOUS

ARCTURUS comes tumbling through the rubble and
scurries to find cover to no avail.

He sees OLIVIA in the car. He tries to get up and run toward her but his legs falter as they turn to ash and crumble along with the rest of him.

Olivia watches his arm reach toward her and puff into dust on the ground.

LIAM hides himself as best as he can, using the spare cloth of a curtain and what's left of his clothing.

He fumbles about, wincing in pain from what is left of the blue sky. Olivia sees him and rushes over to help.

She brings him the sunblock and he applies it to the areas that are now exposed where there was once clothing.

                    LIAM
          I told you to stay in
          the car! There could
          have been another.

                    OLIVIA
          You need help.

                    LIAM
          Yeah, well I don't
          need you dead.

                    OLIVIA
          Same goes for you.

He looks at her. He hasn't had anyone care about his well being in centuries.

                    OLIVIA
          I'll get you my gym
          clothes from the
          trunk.

She runs off to the car, leaving him alone to contemplate.

He looks at the young man hanging upside down, blood dripping from his fingertips. Liam tries to ignore it and avert his eyes.

INT. JAKE'S HOSPITAL ROOM - LAWRENCE GENERAL - NIGHT

There's a muttering. A crack in the voice. A random intonation. A madman's voice. The sound of severe psychological damage.

JAKE suffers from a nightmare.

He jolts awake! Screaming in the night!

MR. and MRS. CUNNINGHAM run in with a NURSE behind them.

                    MRS. CUNNINGHAM
               Oh Jake, honey I'm
               here!

                    MR. CUNNINGHAM
               What's wrong?

                    NURSE
               He only has a case of
               anemia, he should be
               fine!

Jake looks around, wide-eyed. His mother holds him tight.

                    MR. CUNNINGHAM
               You're awake!

                    MRS. CUNNINGHAM
               Oh thank God!

Jake is confused, but embraces his mother.

                    MRS. CUNNINGHAM
               Where were you honey?
               What do you remember?

                    JAKE
          I- I don't remember.
          How did I get here?

                 MR. CUNNINGHAM
          You stumbled into the
          hospital. You've been
          gone a whole day.
          Don't you remember?

Jake shakes his head.

INT. OLIVIA'S HOUSE - OFFICE - NIGHT

OLIVIA searches through an ancestry database
while LIAM looks at a picture of Olivia's mother.

                    LIAM
          That boyfriend of
          yours made it, right?

                   OLIVIA
          Ex, and yes. His mom
          called me.- How do you
          know he won't remember
          anything?

                    LIAM
          It's not possible.
          Arcturus was a master
          alchemist. He became a
          vampire while serving
          as a medicus in the
          Roman Legion. He knew
          how to sedate people,
          and learned to induce
          memory loss.

                   OLIVIA
          - Good. I'd rather
          he didn't know I was
          there.-

Liam knows that a part of her hopes that he'll
be spared the memory of that place; for Jake's

                       94

sake.

Looking at the computer monitor, Olivia shakes her head.

> OLIVIA
> I can't find anything after my great-great grandparents. The only loose ends I see here are an adopted great-great grandmother on my mother's father's side; so, my grandmother's father's mother. Then, there's my Great Grammy. She was raised by her father, and her mother ran off. Also, there's no white people as far as I can see.

> LIAM
> So, your great-great-grandmothers are the best leads we have, then.- And the one who ran off,- who's that?

> OLIVIA
> It doesn't say. There's a random document talking about an arrest. It mentions the name "Mariam Cloud", but I don't know if that's her mother.

PIGEON whines in the doorway leading to the front door.

> OLIVIA
> Oh, okay. I'll take you out.

EXT. OLIVIA'S HOUSE - DRIVEWAY - NIGHT
OLIVIA steps outside with PIGEON and LIAM.

They step off of her porch and into the street.
Pigeon seems to have warmed up to Liam, so Liam
scratches the dog's ears.

MRS. KRAFTON stands on her front lawn, looking
at them.

                    MRS. KRAFTON
          Olivia?

Olivia's heart sinks. How will she explain Liam
to her?

                    OLIVIA
          Mrs. Krafton!

                    MRS. KRAFTON
          How are you sweet-
          heart? Who's the boy?

                    LIAM
          I'm her cousin.

                    MRS. KRAFTON
          Oh good. I thought you
          met him on the inter-
          net.

Olivia blushes.

                    OLIVIA
          Mrs. K! No!

                    MRS. KRAFTON
          Well; as long as
          you're making the
          right decisions. I'm
          glad your cousin is
          here to keep you safe
          while you walk Pi-
          geon.- Hi little Pi-
          geon!

Liam smiles as she slips Pigeon a treat on the sly. Mrs. Krafron then looks at Liam.

> MRS. KRAFTON
> And what's your name, sweetheart?

> LIAM
> I'm Liam. It's a pleasure to meet you.

> MRS. KRAFTON
> Likewise. You like the neighborhood?

> LIAM
> I do! I'm glad to be around family too, so there's always that.

> MRS. KRAFTON
> Is that so?

Olivia is humbled by his remark.

Mrs. Krafton scans Liam on the sly with an inquisitive eye.

> MRS. KRAFTON
> Well I'm glad you guys have each other.

Liam senses her skepticism, and disarms her with a long-lost compliment.

> LIAM
> - You know, there's something very "Kay Francis" about you.

> MRS. KRAFTON
> Oh! Oh my!- Now that's a name I haven't heard in a while.- Where'd you learn a name like that anyway?

Liam smiles while Olivia has no clue what just transpired.

                    MRS. KRAFTON
              Well, thank you dear.
              That's quite the com-
              pliment.- Olivia, hon-
              ey; do me a favor and
              let your mother know I
              say "hello". I've got
              to take care of Spike.

                    OLIVIA
              Will do, Mrs. K! Say
              hello to Spike for me!

Mrs. Krafton walks off to her house, leaving the other three alone in the darkness.

EXT. BARTLET STREET - ANDOVER - CONTINUOUS

OLIVIA and LIAM walk under the warm street-lights on a black night. PIGEON jaunts along on a leash.

Along the road SOMEONE is stapling signs to the telephone poles. They say "BLOOD DRIVE AT ANDO-VER HIGH SCHOOL".

                    LIAM
              I need to ask; why
              didn't you tell your
              mom about the time I
              attacked you?

                    OLIVIA
              I- didn't want to wor-
              ry her.- She's on va-
              cation- and she works
              very hard.

Liam nods. It's understandable, but not healthy for Olivia.

                    LIAM

You're really brave to
stay home alone after
that; but your mother
would want you to tell
her no matter what.

                    OLIVIA
          I know. -It's just
          better to let her be.

                    LIAM
          Is that what was go-
          ing on between you and
          your dad? You didn't
          want to bother him
          with how you felt?

Olivia has never thought about this, but Liam
makes a point.

                    LIAM
          And that ex boyfriend
          of yours. You still
          care about him, but
          you hate to admit it.

                    OLIVIA
          He's a nice guy but-

                    LIAM
          You mean you love
          him; even if you know
          you're not right for
          each other.

Olivia knows he isn't wrong, but she wouldn't
say it that way.

                    OLIVIA
          Like a friend.

                    LIAM
          Believe me, I know.-
          There was a woman af-
          ter my wife died; but
          she wasn't my wife.-

She never could be.

                    OLIVIA
          What is that? If you
          can love people that
          aren't right for you,
          then what makes some-
          one the right one? I
          mean I don't believe
          in a "one" but...

Liam reaches for the words in his mind.

                    LIAM
          It's not "one" but
          "someone". They aren't
          just any old "someone"
          either, but one who
          wouldn't change you
          from the "someone" you
          are. They like you the
          way they found you,
          and they wouldn't have
          it any other way.

Olivia nods.

                    LIAM
          You can only find that
          by being who you are,
          and more important-
          ly, by not trying to
          change who they are.

                    OLIVIA
          What about "working
          together" or "making
          sacrifices"?

Liam puffs out a laugh.

                    LIAM
          When they don't seek
          to change who you are,
          that's making a sacri-
          fice by setting aside
          their ego. That's what

working together is
and you need to be
willing to make that
sacrifice too.

                OLIVIA
Well I can't be a
stay-at-home trophy
wife in the town I
grew up in.

                LIAM
So if he's a small-
town guy and that's
what he wants, -and
that's not you, then
he's not your someone;
and you're not someone
for him either.- You
made the adult deci-
sion and ended it; not
just for your sake,
but his.- Because you
love him.

                OLIVIA
It hurts because he
wants to make it work
and I can't.

                LIAM
That's because he
loves the idea of you,
and not the "someone"
you are.- He might
learn to appreciate
that "someone" some-
day, but that's a mat-
ter of maturity.

Olivia nods. She's never had a conversation so
thorough about her relationship.

                LIAM
Speaking of maturity.-
You know, it's not

changing the "someone"
you are if you learn
new things.

Olivia hears scolding in his tone.

> OLIVIA
> Yeah, I know.

> LIAM
> Well, you'd do good
> to listen.- Because
> you're tough. You get
> it from both your mom
> and your dad.- But
> take my advice.-

Olivia looks him in the eyes.

> LIAM (CONT'D)
> The bravest thing we
> can do is admit how
> we feel; even if it's
> just to ourselves.
> -Nobody likes to think
> of themselves as weak
> or emotional; but it's
> cowardice to turn a
> blind eye on what's
> happening inside. -If
> you can find your way
> through the fog of
> emotions, then you can
> guide yourself out of
> anything.

Olivia can't deny she's been hiding her feelings to everyone around her. She continues her
stride while walking with him.

> OLIVIA
> You haven't met my
> mom. How do you know I
> get that from her?

> LIAM

I'm going off of what
you've said.

She feels this is fair to say with what she's
told him so far.

                    LIAM
          I mean- am I wrong?
          What's she like?

                    OLIVIA
          -Practical, kinda like
          you said.- Not heart-
          less or anything, but
          she's not in your face
          with her feelings.

Liam laughs.

                    LIAM
          Yeah. I figured. -That
          was my wife too. -Of
          all things, of course
          THAT would stand the
          test of time.

                    OLIVIA
          You think it comes
          from her?

                    LIAM
          Definitely. I was al-
          ways pushing for fun
          and excitement. She'd
          say "Liam, yer bark-
          ing up the wrong tree"
          or something.- She
          loved that I did it;
          but she'd be damned if
          she said so.- I mean,
          she'd say things like
          "I like that about ye"
          or "Yer lucky yer so
          sweet to me", but not
          much more than that.

Liam slows his stride as Pigeon stops to pee. He wonders where the time has gone, and feels confident enough to confide an old thought he's never spoken aloud.

> LIAM
> I can't help but feel like all that's happened since then has been my fault.- I pushed to celebrate our anniversary when I should've stayed home.

> OLIVIA
> - Just knowing as little as I do, I don't think it's your fault.- And besides, there's no point in sulking. You've gotta find your daughter. Blaming yourself won't get you any closer.

Liam nods. It's true that blame is pointless.

> LIAM
> I don't get to tell people these thoughts. So- thank you.

> OLIVIA
> You don't talk with ANY people?

> LIAM
> -Living like this,- Everything is like a blur.- Life just passes by and years later you realize the whole world has changed; all the while you were just- hunting, again and again. Trying to

feed yourself while
the world moves on
around you.

Olivia is captivated by this revelation. Mean-
while, Liam is reluctant to say what's next.

                    LIAM
          I must confess.- I've
          gone a hundred years
          before without any
          progress on finding
          Lilly.

                    OLIVIA
          - I thought you did
          that all the time.-
          That's what you do,
          isn't it?

Liam decides she's ready to know the truth;
about this much, at least.

                    LIAM
          I try when I can, but
          there's more to real
          blood than keeping my-
          self young.- There's a
          sensation you get when
          you drink the blood
          of a human.- It's un-
          like anything in the
          world.- You feel pow-
          erful and perfect.-
          Animal blood doesn't
          do that.- It only
          keeps me from rotting,
          like Arcturus did.

                    OLIVIA
          So you've lost time
          because of your need
          to feed.

                    LIAM
          Yes. And it's worse

                    105

                    when the hunger sets
                    in for the first time.
                    After you've turned,
                    you'd do anything for
                    the right blood.-
                    You'd even kill your
                    own family.-

INT. JAKES HOUSE - FRONT DOOR - AFTERNOON

JAKE stands behind and MR. and MRS. CUNNINGHAM
as they enter their house.

A surprise party shouts the usual "surprise!",
and lumbering, Jake can barely feign a reaction.

Everyone is there. His EXTENDED FAMILY and
FRIENDS.

Jake is irritated, feeling unwell, and some
people even comment that he needs to brush his
teeth.

A doctor in the family comments that they'll
need to hold a blood drive to recoup their supply after they saved his life.

INT. JAKES HOUSE - BATHROOM - LATER

JAKE slaps a plate of half-eaten cake next to
the sink. He vomits up the blue frosting.

MRS. CUNNINGHAM knocks on the door.

                    MRS. CUNNINGHAM
                Jake? Are you alright
                in there?

                    JAKE
                Go away Mom! I'm fine!

He's shaking; scared. "Why am I having these
thoughts?" He thinks.

EXT. JAKES BACK YARD - LATER

JAKE steps out to see his own DOG on a leash. He stares at it. The dog is confused.

Someone says his name. He nods in acknowledgement and submerges himself into the shadows. From there, he continues to look at the dog, plotting how he'll get away with it.

INT. JAKES HOUSE - JAKE'S ROOM - LATER

JAKE tosses and turns in his bed, sweating; unable to sleep

He has thoughts enter his mind. A rotten-looking man with an Italian-sounding accent.

INT. ABANDONED BUILDING - LOWER SHAWSHEEN - CONTINUOUS

ARCTURUS uses a nail on his hand to cut into JAKES leg as he hangs upside down.

                    ARCTURUS
          Sometimes, fresh ones
          clean the palate,
          don't you agree?

Arcturus licks the blood, going up the length of the cut.

                    ARCTURUS
          I need to take extra
          care disposing of you,
          but sometimes this is
          worth it.

INT. JAKES HOUSE - FINISHED BASEMENT - LATER

JAKE tries to sit and play video games, but he just can't do it. He stands and paces, tries to sit, but just can't fight his urge.

He's trying so hard to be the person he once was.

"I couldn't possibly do that!" He thinks. "I just can't!"

INT. JAKE'S HOUSE - KITCHEN - LATER

JAKE moans and sways; pained. He's crying. He has a kitchen knife in his hand.

He turns to continue pacing, and he's covered in blood.

                    JAKE
          Mom!

He calls to his mother like she's upstairs. He knows she's not. He calls because he'll never have a reason to do it again.

                    JAKE
          Mom I'm still hungry!

He is sobbing delirious. A delusional denial.

His mother's body is in the hallway leading to the kitchen, directly where Jake can see.

His father's body is slumped in a chair at the kitchen counter.

Jake moves his father's arm, letting it fall; just to see some kind of motion from his father. Any kind.

INT. RETIREMENT HOME - COMMON AREA - DAY

LIAM looks into the vacant expression of Olivia's GREAT-GRANDMOTHER.

                    LIAM
          Mariam Cloud. Mariam.
          Leila.- Lilian.

She stares through him as if he's not there.

                    LIAM
          Aunt Lilly.

OLIVIA stands by her GRANDMOTHER behind Liam, she talks on the phone out of earshot as her grandmother follows along with some unperceived goal.

Liam looks to see if they'll overhear what he's about to do, then back at the great-grand-mother.

His eyes wide, he stares into the depths of her soul like a vampire on an old TV program.

> LIAM
> Look into my eyes. You
> will tell me if you've
> heard the name "Lil-
> ly".

The great-grandmother looks at his expression, acknowledging him for the first time.

> GREAT-GRANDMOTHER
> Are you flirting with
> me?

Liam almost speaks but can't muster a response. He holds back a laugh instead.

> OLIVIA
> What are you doing?

Olivia keeps her voice down and out of her grandmother's hearing range. Her phone slides into her pocket.

> LIAM
> I saw a someone do it
> in a movie once.

> OLIVIA
> Has it ever worked for
> you?

> LIAM
> I've never tried.

109

Olivia fights a smirk.

                    OLIVIA
          Come on. Meet my
          grandmother.

Liam holds a posture of respect.

                    OLIVIA
          Liam, this is my
          grandma. Grammy, this
          is Liam.

                    GRANDMOTHER
          So you're the distant
          relative?

                    LIAM
          Yes. I've been re-
          searching the family
          tree.

                    GRANDMOTHER
          My goodness, you look
          like my cousin Alvin;
          but he died ages ago.-
          He lived to be nine-
          ty-seven, so that must
          be good news for you!

Liam smiles and takes a seat that he's offered.

                    GRANDMOTHER
          So how far back are we
          connected? It has to
          be before my mother.

                    LIAM
          It's sometime be-
          fore that, but I'm not
          sure. That's actually
          what I'm trying to fig-
          ure out.

                    GRANDMOTHER

I wish we could ask my mother. She's not of any help as you can see.

She gestures toward the great-grandmother in the wheelchair.

                    LIAM
          I would've loved to
          ask her so many ques-
          tions. It's okay
          though.

The grandmother shrugs with a crooked mouth.

                    GRANDMOTHER
          Well- it might be okay
          for you; but God won't
          take her and the dev-
          il's afraid she'll
          take over, so I'm
          stuck with her!

                    OLIVIA
          Grandma!

                    GRANDMOTHER
          What? Have a sense of
          humor! My mother would
          have loved that joke.

Her and Liam acknowledge their shared sense of humor with a glance.

                    GRANDMOTHER
          So Olivia says there's
          a certain person
          you're looking for.
          Where our family trees
          split, correct?

                    LIAM
          Yes. This- mutual rel-
          ative should be relat-
          ed to the both of us,

probably a few gener-
ations back. A woman
named Lilly.

The grandmother reaches through her oldest mem-
ories, trying to make the connection. She then
shakes her head.

> GRANDMOTHER
> Never heard of a "Lil-
> ly" in our family.

> LIAM
> Not an aunt, a dis-
> tant cousin; a family
> friend?

> GRANDMOTHER
> I thought this lady
> was supposed to be di-
> rectly related.

> LIAM
> I-. I don't know any-
> more.

The grandmother appraises him for some ulteri-
or motive, but his body language suggests that
this is frustrating for him.

> OLIVIA
> The paperwork on the
> ancestry sight gets
> muddy at that time.

> GRANDMOTHER
> Oh, I see.

> OLIVIA
> How about your grand-
> mother?

> GRANDMOTHER
> Your great-gram-
> my's mother? She left
> without so much as a

"goodbye".
                    OLIVIA
          Could that be Lilly?

               GRANDMOTHER
          Oh, no. Her mother's
          name was Mable.

The great-grandmother hears the loud speaker in
the next room and hums along to "In the Mood"
by Glenn Miller.

                    OLIVIA
          There was some arrest
          document mentioning a
          woman named "Mariam
          Cloud". Does that name
          ring a bell?

               GRANDMOTHER
          My mother might have
          known, but she's long
          past remembering now.

                    OLIVIA
          It's okay Grammy. We
          really appreciate your
          help.

               GRANDMOTHER
          Well of course, dear;
          and if I remember any-
          thing, I'll phone you.
          I promise.

                    OLIVIA
          Thank you Grandma. I
          appreciate it.

I/E. OLIVIA'S CAR - RETIREMENT HOME - LATER

OLIVIA and LIAM stand at the front of the car.

                    OLIVIA
          So I think that rules
          out Great-Grammy's

                    113

mother. We'll have to
follow up on the or-
phan; on Grandma's
dad's side.

> LIAM
> Your great-grandmother
> has my blood. It's her
> side for sure. It has
> to be.

> OLIVIA
> You want to dig deeper
> there?

> LIAM
> -She didn't recognize
> any of the names; but
> a name should trigger
> SOME recognition.

> OLIVIA
> Liam, she wouldn't
> recognize her own
> daughter's name if you
> said it to her.

Liam surrenders. Olivia would know better than
him. She probably IS that far gone.

> OLIVIA
> What about Great-Gran-
> nie's husband?

> LIAM
> It's HER who has my
> blood.

> OLIVIA
> What if, while she
> was pregnant, she
> shared her blood with
> her baby in the womb.
> Maybe that's how it
> works. I don't know,
> I'm trying to help.

Liam sighs.

                    LIAM
          I have a feeling Lilly
          lived and died a long
          time ago.

                    OLIVIA
          Just hold on be-
          fore you draw a con-
          clusion.- Get in the
          trunk. We've got some-
          where to be.

Liam sighs and moves toward the back.

I/E. OLIVIA'S CAR - CEMETARY ENTRANCE - NIGHT

OLIVIA stops the car, moves to the back seat,
and opens the back to the trunk space.

                    OLIVIA
          So, to catch you up
          to speed, Great-Gran-
          nie's husband was
          buried here at this
          cemetery. His moth-
          er's name was Lillian
          Lee. She died ages ago
          with no record of her
          parentage.- She was
          tried for suspicion
          of grave robbery, il-
          legal trade of goods,
          and breaking an entry.
          She was a curator of
          historical artifacts
          with questionable or-
          igins. Findings indi-
          cated that none of her
          goods were ill-gotten
          and all charges were
          dropped.

                    LIAM
          Sounds promising.

                    OLIVIA
          Do you want to see the
          grave?
                    LIAM
          I might have to do a
          little more than see
          it.-

Olivia doesn't understand what he means; but he
looks at her until she gets the memo.

Her adrenaline kicks in.

EXT. GRAVEYARD - GREAT GRANDFATHER'S GRAVE -
LATER

OLIVIA and LIAM approach the tombstone. They
stand and stare a while in silence.

                    OLIVIA
          Are you gonna need
          anything?

                    LIAM
          No. -I'll see you at
          the house. I can do
          this alone.

Olivia leaves feeling like an accomplice. He
looks around the area. There's a shed. He walks
there to get a shovel.

INT. LIAM'S COTTAGE - CHILDREN'S BEDROOM -
NIGHT 1710

LIAM tucks LILLY in.

                    LIAM
          I'm gonna close the
          door tonight. Will you
          be okay?

                    LILLY
          I'm scared to, Da'.

                    LIAM
          Don't you be scared
          of nothin'. No matter
          what, yer dad won't
          let some monster take
          ye from him.

EXT. GRAVEYARD - GREAT GRANDFATHER'S GRAVE -
PRESENT

LIAM looks down at the handkerchief in hand.

                    LIAM
          It'll all be over
          soon.

He lifts the shovel and SLAMS the spade into
the ground!

He stomps it in further!

EXT. BACK YARD - NEIGHBOR'S HOUSE - NIGHT

JAKE is licking the blood from a dog carcass.

Around the corner, in the light of a sliding
door's window, an OLD WOMAN steps outside.

                  OLD WOMAN
          Bruiser! Bruiser you
          need to come in boy!

The dog doesn't respond. It doesn't show up
wiggling and wagging. Not a sound.

She turns the corner to see if her dog is
there. On the grass she sees the mutilated body
of her pet, limbs going awkward directions.
She's in shock and backs away.

CLAP on her mouth! Jake's other hand squeez-
es her throat and he rips her jaw out! He tries
to catch every drop in his mouth as blood spews
out. Her gurgling is hushed by his haste.

EXT. GRAVEYARD - GREAT GRANDFATHER'S GRAVE -
NIGHT

LIAM opens the coffin. The great-grandfather's
body is laid bare to the sky.
To the side of the body, there's an old ring. A
Celtic knot with an emerald in the middle.

Liam remembers it on his wife's hand all those
years ago.

This is it.

The worst.

She lived as a vampire, and died without seeing
her father again.

He's failed.

INT. OLIVIA'S HOUSE - KITCHEN - NIGHT

OLIVIA is with PIGEON at the kitchen counter.
She eats a sandwich while a dial-tone rings on
her cellphone.

Pigeon waits to watch TV with her.

                    LIONEL
                  (o.s.)
             Hey honey, how are
             you?

                    OLIVIA
             I'm alright. Did you
             fly home okay?

                    LIONEL
                  (o.s.)
             Yeah! Just picked up
             Linguisa from the ken-
             nel.

Linguisa barks on the other end of the phone.

                    LIONEL
                    (o.s.)
          Ah! Damned wiener
          dog!- Why you calling?
          Don't tell me you're
          having trouble sleep-
          ing.-
Olivia laughs.

                    OLIVIA
          No Dad-

                    LIONEL
                    (o.s.)
          If you tell your mom
          I traumatized you at
          that haunted house I-

                    OLIVIA
          Dad!

                    LIONEL
                    (o.s.)
          What?

                    OLIVIA
          I called because I
          wanted to say I miss
          you.

                    LIONEL
                    (o.s.)
          - You expect me to be-
          lieve that?- You know,
          it's not just moms
          that can pick up when
          something's up.

Olivia sighs.

                    OLIVIA
          Well, I did think of
          something recently,
          but- I don't mean any-
          thing by asking you.

                    119

                    LIONEL
                    (o.s.)
              Ask away sweetheart.
Olivia drags up the question from deep within.

                    OLIVIA
              Well, you know I broke
              up with Jake and all-
              and- going through a
              breakup had me wonder-
              ing- why did you do
              what you did to mom?-
              I'm not blaming you,
              but I mean, you know
              it was wrong.- And I
              don't want you to sug-
              ar-coat the answer. I
              want to know for my
              own relationships- in
              the future, you know?

                    LIONEL
                    (o.s.)
              Well, tha-. That's
              a great question to
              be asking. And- you
              SHOULD ask. You have
              the right to know.- I
              just don't think I re-
              ally have an answer.-
              I don't really under-
              stand it myself, but I
              haven't been able to
              stay still my whole
              life.- Ever since I
              was a kid; the nuns
              used to hit me 'cause
              I'd cause trouble.- I
              just, don't know how
              to behave. I just-
              don't know.

                    OLIVIA
              Do you think you love
              mom, but you're just

                       120

not made for each oth-
er?

                    LIONEL
                     (o.s.)
That's probably- the
best way to put it,
Olivia. You're wise
beyond your years, and
that's a trait of your
mother's that I love.
-And you know some-
thing, I'd say I'd do
things differently if
I could go back in
time, but I know I'd
mess it up again.- I'm
sorry to admit that,
but it's true. -And
I'll probably never be
lucky enough to meet
someone like your mom
again, and I'm happy
she likes the new guy
she's with. Don't ever
settle for somebody
like me, Olivia.

                    OLIVIA
I'll do my best.

Lionel detects the sarcasm and laughs.

                    LIONEL
                     (o.s.)
Well, you keep to
that.- And Olivia-

                    OLIVIA
Yeah?

                    LIONEL
                     (o.s.)
I might not be able to
go back and do right
by your mom; but I can

                    121

do right by you now.-
You're my daughter.
That's different.
                    OLIVIA
I know Dad. Thank you
for the honesty.

                    LIONEL
          (o.s.)
Anytime honey. I've
gotta wake up ear-
ly tomorrow. -Are you
good?

                    OLIVIA
I am.

                    LIONEL
(o.s.)
Okay. You have a good
night. Your mom should
be home early tomor-
row. She just texted
me.

                    OLIVIA
I know. I love you
dad.

                    LIONEL
          (o.s.)
I love you too. Bye
honey.

                    OLIVIA
Bye.

Olivia hangs up. Pigeon looks off to the door.

A figure comes to the side door that opens to
the kitchen, activating an automatic porch
light.

The light goes out. The figure unscrewed the
bulb.

122

The doorbell rings.

Olivia spins around! She's careful not to make
a sound as she gets up and looks at the time.
Liam couldn't possibly be home.
She moves to the side of the door. Pigeon is
barking.

The figure on the other side is completely in
shadow. Olivia can't see who it is.

She picks up a knife and shuts off the kitchen
light.

                    OLIVIA
          Hello?

There's no response. Just someone on the other
side, plotting.

                    OLIVIA
          Who's there?

                    JAKE
          Olivia, can I come in?

                    OLIVIA
          Jake?

                    JAKE
          - Is your mom home,
          Olivia?

He's said her name twice. It feels unnatural to
her.

                    OLIVIA
          Yes, she is.

                    JAKE
          Oh. I was hoping we
          could talk.- Something
          happened to me re-
          cently and it had me
          thinking; I -I wanna
          try again.

                    OLIVIA
          Jake, we went over
          this.

                    JAKE
          I'll go anywhere with
          you Olivia. I don't
          care where it is. I
          want you to live out
          your dreams, -and I
          want to be there to
          see you happy.

JAKE is eager to make his way in. His eyes
twinkle with a night vision glow like an ani-
mal. His smile is dripping with blood in the
darkness.

Olivia can't see him. He's perfectly disguised
by the streetlight behind him.

                    JAKE
          You were right. Would
          you let me in to say
          this in person? It'll
          only take a minute.

She sees that the door is unlocked, and the
switch for the automatic light is on. She moves
the switch; off, then on, being careful not to
make a sound. Still, there's no light.

                    OLIVIA
          Why'd you ask if my
          mom was home?

                    JAKE
          I didn't see her car
          here.

Olivia is realizing the full picture of what's
happened.

                    OLIVIA
          It's in the shop.

                    124

                    JAKE
          Oh, I didn't know
          that.

Olivia moves her hand to lock the door.
It makes a "clink!" and Jake notices.

He tries the door knob. It's not moving. He
tries his best to stay composed but tries multiple times with force.

                    OLIVIA
          We can talk tomorrow
          at the café.

He has to change tactics. She suspects him.
He holds his head and begins to make a crying
face.

                    JAKE
          Olivia?

                    OLIVIA
          What?

                    JAKE
          - I was also wondering
          if you had anything.-
          You see, I fell and I
          hit my head real bad.-
          I'm bleeding a lot.

Olivia's heart sinks. She backs away.

                    JAKE
          It hurts really bad
          Olivia. I need your
          help. -Please?

He keeps asking again and again, then stops.

Olivia watches as he moves away from the door.

She realizes something.

                      125

She BOLTS out of the room!

INT. OLIVIA'S HOUSE - LIVING ROOM - CONTINUOUS
OLIVIA rushes to check all the windows and shut
the curtains.
She stops to think a moment.

She looks up the stairs.

His footsteps clomp in a stride on the porch.

She looks for him through another window, but
sees nothing. She then looks up at the ceiling.

EXT. OLIVIA'S HOUSE - FRONT PORCH - CONTINUOUS

He looks in through a window on the roof of the
porch.

His limbs are spread like a spider on the sid-
ing of the house.

He turns his ear to the house to listen through
the walls.

A window opens, then slam shut!

Footsteps in the back of the house.

He hears the footsteps going toward the neighbor's shed.

A crashing in the same direction.

He grins to himself.

INT. MRS. KRAFTON'S HOUSE - CONTINUOUS

MRS. KRAFTON springs up off the couch!

SPIKE barks at the back door!

Through the back window, she sees a hint of
movement. A shadow cast across her yard from
Olivia's back yard light.

                    MRS. KRAFTON
                  Son of a bitch!

Mrs. Krafton opens a closet where a shotgun
stands ready. She looks at a photo of her late
husband.

                    MRS. KRAFTON
                  Let's hope I don't see
                  you anytime too soon,
                  Homer.

Spike whines, wanting to join her.

                    MRS. KRAFTON
                  You stay here. You
                  have a lot more years
                  left than I do.

Spike is worried for her as she leaves through
the back door.

INT. MRS. KRAFTON'S SHED - ENTRY WAY - CONTINU-
OUS

JAKE enters the shed and sees a ladder with a
broken rung going to a crawlspace.

A spot full of clutter to hide behind, but
she's trapped up there.

He walks in, looking up.

INT. DARK SPACE - CONTINUOUS

OLIVIA hides somewhere in the dark.

INT. MRS. KRAFTON'S SHED - ENTRY WAY - CONTINU-
OUS

JAKE smiles and moves in to find his victim.

He steps near the ladder, almost taunting her
in his approach.

Just as his hand reaches the rung, he's

grabbed!

He's ripped off his feet!
A spin!

CRACK!

The stake made from the broken ladder rung breaks through his ribcage!

His heart protrudes from his chest!

It's skewered at the end of the stake!

LIAM looks him in the eyes.

He glares at him, almost as if to say "Amateur".

Jake begins to dry into a husk of a human form. His heart does the same. It looks like a spent piece of coal.

His body crumbles into dust under its own weight.

Liam wraps his hand around the heart and crushes it, making his fingers wrap around the stake. He brings his chest to the tip.

He looks down at it. He longs to rest.

                    MRS. KRAFTON
              Don't fuckin' move!-
              Or I'll blast you
              straight to Hell!

MRS. KRAFTON comes around the corner with her shotgun pointed at Liam.

                    LIAM
              Mrs. K, was it? I'm so
              sorry.

                    MRS. KRAFTON
              What the hell are you

doing in here?!-

Mrs. Krafton knocks over some things on the wall. She's cut on the leg with a rake.

Liam can smell it. The craving comes in a wave.

>   MRS. KRAFTON
>   Son of a gun!- Tell me
>   what you're doing in
>   MY SHED!

>   LIAM
>   Miss, I would really
>   prefer if you didn't
>   block the exit. I
>   think Olivia can clear
>   this up.

>   MRS. KRAFTON
>   Are you really that
>   girl's cousin?!

Liam is fighting the urge with everything he has.

>   MRS. KRAFTON
>   Well! Are you?!

EXT. MRS. KRAFTON'S BACK YARD - CONTINUOUS

MRS. KRAFTON's shadow is cast against the curtain in the window.

Her silhouette engulfed by LIAM's!

SMASH! Gardening tools tumble from the walls!

INT. OLIVIA'S HOUSE - OFFICE - CONTINUOUS

OLIVIA hides in a dark corner behind a desk. She holds a kitchen knife.

The desk is moved. LIAM looks down at her. He hides his thoughts behind a plain face.

                    LIAM
          He won't be coming
          back.
                    OLIVIA
          Is he dead?

                    LIAM
          He died the other
          day.- All I did was
          put him to rest.

Olivia looks him over. He's covered in dirt.

For a loss of words, she plops down in a chair.

                    OLIVIA
          What happened at the
          grave?

Liam hands her the ring.

                    LIAM
          Don't worry, I washed
          it.- It was a gift I
          gave to my wife.- Lil-
          ly was probably a vam-
          pire. She lived and
          passed away a long
          time ago.- If I hadn't
          wasted my time, then I
          would have been there
          for her. If I was
          there, then she'd know
          that I never gave up
          on her.

                    OLIVIA
          You don't know that
          for sure-

                    LIAM
          Oh please! What other
          option is there?

Pigeon cowers away from Liam. He looks long at
Pigeon.

Olivia bolts up to stand between them.

                    LIAM
          Give me the keys to
          your car.

                    OLIVIA
          Why?

                    LIAM
          I'm going to hunt.
          I'll be at the woods
          near the hill.

                    OLIVIA
          You'll be right back?

                    LIAM
          If I'm not, then that
          means I've lost con-
          trol.- And if that
          happens, then you'll
          never see me again, I
          promise.

                    OLIVIA
          You won't lose con-
          trol.- You wouldn't.

                    LIAM
          Well- if I do, then
          keep that ring.

                    OLIVIA
          Stop talking like
          that. You haven't even
          met my mom yet-

                    LIAM
          It belongs to the fam-
          ily!

She's never seen him so emotional. He's impos-
sible to communicate with. At the same time,
she's touched by how defensive he is; for their

sake.

He puts his hand out for the keys, and she hands them over.

                    OLIVIA
          Just to Holt Hill;
          then back.

He looks long at Olivia, trying to find some last words to say.

                    LIAM
          I'm proud of you.

It's all he can manage to say.

With that, and not another word, he leaves.

EXT. HOLT HILL - ANDOVER - DAWN

By the parked car, LIAM looks at the animals in the distance. Even with his hunger, he ignores them.

He walks to the front of the car and takes a lighter to some kindling, then looks out over the land surrounding the hill.

In the fire, Liam burns his fake I.D.s, a library card, a marked up map, some credit cards, and finally, he pulls out the handkerchief.

EXT. LAKESIDE - TWO-HUNDRED YEARS AGO - EVENING

LIAM looks at the woman in the BLUE DRESS as she puts out her clean hand, smirking like she was before.

She places the handkerchief neatly into her bosom.

                    BLUE DRESS
          I can talk if you have
          a while to spare. Help
          me over this rock if

you could?

Liam takes her hand and boosts her up from the rocky shores but she slips and cuts her foot.

                    BLUE DRESS
          Ah! These damned
          rocks!

She grabs her leg in pain, then notices how still he is.

She sees his face; still and open-mouthed.

She touches his cheek. She likes him.

                    BLUE DRESS
          Oh, it's just a
          scratch and it happens
          all the time. It's not
          your fault so don't
          blame yourself. Why my
          father-

She sees his face. Still unmoved. Unchanged.

She laughs her nerves away.

                    BLUE DRESS
          It's just a bit of
          bloo-.

He attacks!

EXT. HOLT HILL - ANDOVER - DAWN

LIAM looks down at the rag as it burns in the fire. He has no choice but to let it go. The hair oil she used is long gone. It lost that smell many years ago. To anyone else, it's just an old rag.

He breathes like a curse has been lifted in the act he is committing.

He removes his jacket. The sky brightens as the

sun begins to rise.

He sits on the front of the car.
It'll be the first sunrise he's seen in a long
time.

INT. LIAM'S COTTAGE - CHILDREN'S BEDROOM -
MORNING 1711

LIAM remembers waking LILLY to watch the sunrise.

The TWINS rub their eyes with the backs of
their fists.

INT. LIAM'S COTTAGE - LIAM'S BEDROOM - MORNING
1711

Liam remembers his WIFE smiling at him with
their infant son between them. The sunshine on
her face, he can see it clearly again, and the
little ball of life between them.

She hums her lullaby to their infant child.

EXT. OLIVIA'S HOUSE - DRIVEWAY - MORNING

LIAM watches from the woods across the street.
OLIVIA'S MOTHER leaves for work while OLIVIA
carries her backpack to school.

INT. RETIREMENT HOME - COMMON AREA - DAY

LIAM looks into the face of the old
GREAT-GRANDMOTHER as she smiles. He turns to
see OLIVIA and the GRANDMOTHER in conversation.

He looks back at the very old woman. The last
time he saw her, she was singing Glenn Miller's
'In The Mood'.

EXT. HOLT HILL - ANDOVER - DAWN

The sun is up.

INT. OLIVIA'S HOUSE - OLIVIA'S ROOM - MORNING

OLIVIA wakes up, remembering the night before.

She lifts herself out of bed. A memory comes to her mind.

She rushes to the window!

Her car isn't in there.

EXT. WOODLAND PATH - ANDOVER - DAY

OLIVIA races on a bicycle!

She pedals as fast as she can to the hill!

EXT. HOLT HILL - ANDOVER - MORNING

OLIVIA drops her bike.

She races to the hood of the car!

There's no one there!

A jacket on the hood of the car.

At the front of the hood, there's a pile of ashes.

Her knees grow weak and she fights the tears but can't. She starts to cry.

She leans against the car. On the floor she finds the keys.

She uses them to open the door and sits in the driver's seat.

She feels defeated. She tosses the jacket into the passenger's seat.

She gathers herself together and turns the car on.

A knocking comes from the back seat.

Olivia turns and looks toward the back. The knocking comes again.

She turns the car off.

> OLIVIA
> Liam?

> LIAM
> (o.s.)
> It's me!

She moves to the back of the car and opens the seat.

She throws the jacket in. She fumbles to grab another thing, then throws in what's left of the sunblock at LIAM.

> OLIVIA
> There's not much sun-
> block left! I'll get
> you more!- Liam what
> were you THINKING?!

> LIAM
> -When I came after
> you behind the gro-
> cery store, it wasn't
> to get a closer look.
> -I've hurt innocent
> people when I've lost
> control. -I can't keep
> going on, losing con-
> trol then finding my-
> self again.

> OLIVIA
> So you go and do
> this?!

> LIAM
> I didn't-

> OLIVIA
> Don't do that ever

again!- I don't care
if you've slipped up
in the past, you need
to try!

Liam appears defeated.

> OLIVIA
> You can stay on animal
> blood. I'll help you
> find Lilly; and if you
> don't find her in time,
> you can live out the
> rest of your life with
> us.- If we find her af-
> ter you've lived your
> life, we'll tell her
> everything you've done
> for her.- Liam, you
> don't have to do this
> alone anymore.

Liam cries a watery tear of blood.

> LIAM
> But what about all the
> bad things I've done.

She sighs at his pitiful state.

> OLIVIA
> - You might not be
> able to go back and
> right your wrongs;
> but you can do good
> with the time you have
> left. Grammy would
> say "Be a servant of
> God and he'll forgive
> you".

Liam leans over into her arms and she embraces
him in a hug.

She sighs with relief.

Liam talks into her shoulder.

> LIAM
> Your great-grand-
> mother.- How old is
> she?

Liam backs away to look at her, and Olivia
tries to recall Great-Grammy's age.

> OLIVIA
> She just turned a hun-
> dred and two.

> LIAM
> - Really?

> OLIVIA
> Grammy wasn't joking.
> The big guy won't take
> her.

> LIAM
> Something- something's
> up with that.- I have
> an idea.

> POLICE OFFICER
> (o.s.)
> Excuse me, ma'm!

Olivia moves out of the car and closes the back
seat in one motion.

She looks at the POLICE OFFICER who pulled up
behind the car.

> POLICE OFFICER
> You're not allowed
> here until sun up.
> How'd you get this car
> up anyway?

> OLIVIA
> I drove it. The road

was open.

                POLICE OFFICER
          Can I ask what it is
          you're doing?

                OLIVIA
          I've been going
          through a lot. Just
          needed a place to
          clear my head.

The police officer moves to see what's inside
the car.

                POLICE OFFICER
          Do you have a license
          and registration,
          miss?

                OLIVIA
          I do. Let me grab it
          for you.

Olivia gives the man her paperwork and he stops
just short of going to his vehicle.

                POLICE OFFICER
          Do you have anything
          on you?

                OLIVIA
          No, sir.

                POLICE OFFICER
          If I asked you to open
          your trunk, would I
          find anything illegal
          in there?

                OLIVIA
          No, absolutely not.

                POLICE OFFICER
          Why were you accessing

your trunk?

                    OLIVIA
          Uhm.- Well, I-

The police officer appraises her reaction.

                    OLIVIA
          There's feminine prod-
          ucts in there. It's a
          little embarrassing.

                    POLICE OFFICER
          I'm going to need you
          to open that trunk
          when I get back. Don't
          move.

The police officer goes toward his cruiser and
Olivia worries for Liam.

INT. TRUNK - OLIVIA'S CAR - CONTINUOUS

Liam applies as much sunblock as he can.

EXT. HOLT HILL - ANDOVER - CONTINUOUS

The police officer is in his cruiser for a moment. He dials a number on his personal phone.
He then hears the RADIO.

                    RADIO
          We have a multiple ho-
          micide in a house on
          High Plain Road. All
          available units please
          respond.

The officer is stunned. These things are growing
more prevalent in this otherwise quiet town.

The person he's called picks up.

                    POLICE OFFICER
          Hey, it's me.

                       140

Olivia is frozen; waiting for the officer. She can't hear anything he's saying from where she stands.

INT. TRUNK - OLIVIA'S CAR - CONTINUOUS

Liam runs out of sunblock and it's not enough.

EXT. HOLT HILL - ANDOVER - CONTINUOUS

The officer returns with her paperwork.

                    POLICE OFFICER
          So you're a good
          friend of my sister's.
          She says you play the
          trumpet pretty well.

The officer looks to the front of the car and sees the ash pile.

He looks at Olivia and huffs his disappointment.

                    POLICE OFFICER
          Are you kidding?

He moves closer to inspect and looks at her in silence.

                    OLIVIA
          I just.- They're cer-
          tain things I wanted
          to get rid of.

                    POLICE OFFICER
          Olivia, I don't care
          what the hell you're
          going through. Don't
          do that again.

                    OLIVIA
          I promise I won't,
          sir.

                    POLICE OFFICER
          And don't go on prop-
          erties you're not sup-
          posed to.

                    OLIVIA
          I won't.

The officer walks back toward his car but stops
half way, looking at the trunk.

                    POLICE OFFICER
          Nothing's going on
          here?

                    OLIVIA
          Nothing at all. I'm
          sorry sir.

                    POLICE OFFICER
          Don't sweat it. Kaylie
          sends her regards from
          the hospital.

                    OLIVIA
          Oh my god. You're Kay-
          lie's brother?

                    POLICE OFFICER
          I am.

                    OLIVIA
          How is she? Does she
          seem okay?

                    POLICE OFFICER
          Yeah- but we haven't
          told anyone about her
          condition.-

                    OLIVIA
          Oh, I just meant; I
          haven't seen her in so
          long and you say she's
          in the hospital.

                    POLICE OFFICER
          - She was found pret-
          ty banged up. Bare-
          ly alive.- Don't tell
          anyone, please.

                    OLIVIA
          I wouldn't dream of
          it. Would she mind if
          I come see her some-
          time?

                    POLICE OFFICER
          - I think that might
          be good for her.

                    OLIVIA
          I'll reach out and see
          if I can stop by.

                    POLICE OFFICER
          I'll let her know.-
          Please stay out of
          trouble.

                    OLIVIA
          I will.

The officer drives away and Olivia breathes
again.

I/E. OLIVIA'S HOUSE - CAR IN DRIVEWAY - DAY

OLIVIA runs out of the house with sunblock,
then opens the car door and the back seat. LIAM
looks out at her with a pained face.

                    OLIVIA
          Here. You should be
          able to cover up with
          the rest of this.

                    LIAM
          We have a bigger prob-
          lem.

                    143

                    OLIVIA
          W-what's that?

                    LIAM
          I didn't feed myself
          last night.

                    OLIVIA
          Oh Jesus. What do I
          do?

                    LIAM
          I'll need to get some
          big animals. I've been
          a long time without
          food.

                    OLIVIA
          What about my blood?

                    LIAM
          No!

                    OLIVIA
          I could just-

                    LIAM
          Absolutely not!

                    OLIVIA
          Well, would human
          blood work better than
          a few big animals?

                    LIAM
          I'm not killing any-
          one.

                    OLIVIA
          That's nice but it
          wasn't my question.

                    LIAM
          -Yes. It would help.

                    OLIVIA

                    Alright. I have an
                    idea, then.

She shuts the back seat closed.

EXT. ANDOVER HIGH SCHOOL - PARKING LOT - LATER

OLIVIA pulls her car into a space near the theater. Signs point toward the Field House saying
"BLOOD DRIVE: THIS WAY".

She speaks to LIAM through the seat.

                    OLIVIA
              I'm going to be a
              while! I need to avoid
              the cameras in the
              school, but I'll be
              right back! Stay put!

INT. CAR TRUNK - CONTINUOUS

LIAM is in pain. His limbs are undergoing rigor
mortis and his head hurts from a dehydration of
blood.

I/E. ANDOVER HIGH SCHOOL - PARKING LOT - CON-
TINUOUS

OLIVIA's phone buzzes and sees that her text
didn't go through to her mother. It says "Hey
mom. Call me when you can."

                    OLIVIA
              Oh God. I've gotta
              make this quick!

EXT. OLIVIA'S HOUSE - DRIVEWAY - DAY

PATRICIA starts unloading things from her car
when MRS. KRAFTON comes up the driveway.

                    MRS. KRAFTON
                 Patricia!

                    PATRICIA

145

Hey Mrs. Krafton! How
are you?

                MRS. KRAFTON
          I'm well, how was your
          vacation?

                PATRICIA
          It was alright. Just
          a weekend in Vermont.
          Nothing too fancy; or
          expensive for that
          matter.

                MRS. KRAFTON
          I don't blame you.
          Things are too expen-
          sive these days.- Hey,
          do me a favor and tell
          your nephew I'm sor-
          ry for pointing that
          gun at him the other
          night.

Olivia's mom feels her blood boil.

                PATRICIA
          Nephew?

                MRS. KRAFTON
          The white gentleman
          who went looking for
          Pigeon in my shed last
          night.- He pulled me
          out of the way before
          my gardening tools
          came CRASHING down!
          He's a really nice
          boy.

Patricia is fuming!

                PATRICIA
          Oh I bet!

INT. COLLINS CENTER - BACK DOOR - CONTINUOUS

OLIVIA sees THEATER KIDS scurrying around and
TEACHERS organizing for a school play.
A girl named RACHEL sees her.

                    RACHEL
              Olivia!

Olivia signals her to be quiet, and Rachel lowers her volume.

                    RACHEL (CONT'D)
              You're not supposed to
              be back here. I'm glad
              you came to see the
              show-

                    OLIVIA
              I'm sorry, Rachel. I'm
              not here for the play.
              I- forgot something in
              my locker.

                    RACHEL
              Oh, I don't think
              they'll let you in
              from this side. The
              rest of the school is
              closed except for here
              and the blood drive;
              but that's on the oth-
              er side of the school
              in the field house.
              Maybe you can ask
              someone over there to
              walk you to your lock-
              er.

Olivia sighs.

                    OLIVIA
              Thank you Rachel. I'll
              give it a shot.

Olivia pretends to leave, and as soon as Rachel
has turned her back, Olivia ducks into a door-

way.

Through a small room, Olivia reaches an open back-stage area for props and fabricating. She knows a little secret here from summer school.

The sound of footsteps tap into earshot from around a corner ahead.

Olivia jumps!

She climbs up a small ledge and in the chaos a broom falls over.

Two TEACHERS walk around the corner and look at the broom.

> TEACHER 1
> Is somebody there?

Olivia scrambles into a crawlspace that travels through a dark space between ceiling tiles and the roof of the hallway.

INT. COLLINS CENTER - SCAFFOLDING - CONTINUOUS

The stage of the theater is empty before the show, and OLIVIA stands on a hidden balcony to the side of the great room.

The tapping of approaching feet grows louder from the previous room.

Olivia races up a ladder to the side!

The ladder reaches up the side of the auditorium until it reaches a lone scaffolding that stretches across the width of the room.

At the very top, Olivia scrambles to the top JUST in time! A head pokes out of the hole below and looks up the ladder, but Olivia lays just out of their sight.

After waiting a moment, she hears the person leave. Olivia then moves to walk across the scaffolding.

Along the way, she stops at the sight of something carved into the paint on a support beam.
It's a heart with "Olivia + Jake" in the middle. Underneath it reads "2010".

Olivia feels this with her fingers and the
weight of Jake's death bears down on her.

                    TEAHCER 2
                Hey! Up there!

Olivia doesn't even look at the teacher but
RUNS!

She gets to the other side.

It's another ladder.

She rushes down, even sliding down the end.

Across another dark tunnel she makes her way to
a classroom.

Using an adjoining door, she slips into the
next class unnoticed, and the teachers come
rushing in after she's gone.

INT. ADJOINING CLASSROOM - CONTINUOUS

OLIVIA glides into the main hall and past the
ticket booth. The sight of other adults makes
her pretend to react to the panicked teachers.

Once she's passed the adults, she slides into
another hallway, leading to the main building
of the high school.

INT. COLLINS CENTER HALL - MEDIA CENTER - CON-
TINUOUS

OLIVIA passes the T.V. production studio and
slides into a little-known door.

INT. DIRT ROOM - CONTINUOUS

OLIVIA comes into the room where two HORMONAL
TEENS are making out.
They stop what they're doing and look embar-
rassed at Olivia.

> OLIVIA
> Sorry. Just passing
> through.

Olivia slides into the next room where she sees
an abandoned desk in the dark and fabled "dirt
room".

On the desk, she finds an old hair-tie of hers.

> OLIVIA
> Damn it. I've been
> looking everywhere
> for-

She pockets the hair-tie and sees movement
through the cafeteria kitchen.

NURSES are moving around the area beyond the
doorway, and in the light of the next room she
can see bags of blood being brought into a
walk-in fridge.

Olivia moves into the kitchen and tucks away in
a corner where the nurses won't notice her.

> NURSE
> I just want to thank
> you all for helping us
> today.

> COOK
> Not a problem at all.

> NURSE
> We'll sanitize the
> fridge when we're all
> done.

> COOK

Oh thank you. And of
course, anything you
need. Those two miss-
ing kids must have
done a number on the
blood supply. You guys
saved their lives.
We can't repay you
enough-

The voices trail off and Olivia thinks the
coast is clear. She moves into the hall.

NURSE 2 comes around the corner, looking at
some papers in his hands.

Olivia slides onto the fridge before it closes.

Nurse 2 thinks he saw something out of the corner of his eye. He moves toward the fridge to
examine.

INT. WALK-IN FRIDGE - CONTINUOUS

OLIVIA sees the blood pouches lining the
shelves along the walls.

She takes a few into her bag and zips it up.
Then, the door opens!

NURSE 2 walks in and sees nothing out of the
ordinary.

Behind a box of uncut melons and cantaloupes,
Olivia hides out of sight.

Her phone buzzes.

Her mother is calling.

She silences it!

The Nurse 2 believes he heard it, over by the
melons.

NURSE 1 comes in.

151

                    NURSE 1
          The hell are you do-
          ing?

                    NURSE 2
          I thought I saw some-
          one come in here.

                    NURSE 1
          You saw someone?

                    NURSE 2
          Well no, I thought I
          did.- I was doing pa-
          perwork.

                    NURSE 1
          You're probably just
          seeing things.

                    NURSE 2
          Yeah but, I could have
          sworn I put two bags
          of blood here. Both O
          positive.

                    NURSE 1
          Well I don't see any-
          thing here now.

                    NURSE 2
          Yeah but I have a sys-
          tem to this and it's
          all out of place.
          There should be two
          bags there.

                    NURSE 1
          Who do you think is
          robbing this place?
          We're not exactly run-
          ning that kind of a
          bank.

Nurse 1 walks out of the fridge but Nurse 2

looks around a little more, nearly peering behind the boxes of melons.

Nurse 1 yanks the door open again!

                    NURSE 2
          Come on! I'm starving.
          I don't wanna wait all
          day for you.

                    NURSE 1
          Alright! Alright! I'm
          coming!

Both nurses leave the fridge and Olivia emerges
from behind the boxes.

EXT. ANDOVER HIGH SCHOOL - PARKING LOT - LATER

OLIVIA walks out of the school and sees GIRL 3.

                    GIRL 3
          Olivia!

                    OLIVIA
          Hey!

                    GIRL 3
          You heard? They found
          Jake!

                    OLIVIA
          Yeah, I know.-

                    GIRL 3
          Are you relieved to
          know he's alright?

                    OLIVIA
          Yeah- I am.

                    GIRL 3
          Is that why you were
          here? To donate blood?

                    OLIVIA

No. I forgot my text-
book in my locker.

                    GIRL 3
          Damn girl. That's why
          no one uses lockers.

                    OLIVIA
          I've started making it
          my own little bubble,
          but maybe I should
          give up the habit.

                    GIRL 3
          Oh, by the way. Did
          you do the reading as-
          signment they handed
          out in english class?

                    OLIVIA
          Oh I got that out of
          the way.

                    GIRL 3
          Do you have it on you?

                    OLIVIA
          Yeah. I've got it in
          my-

                    GIRL 3
          Can I have your copy?

Olivia's face turns blank. The packet is directly next to two blood packs in her bag.

                    OLIVIA
          Uh-. I think I don't
          have it- On me.

Girl 3 laughs at her uncertainty.

                    GIRL 3
          You think? Or you just
          don't?
                    OLIVIA

                    I mean I don't. I uh-.

There's an awkward silence but it's broken.
GIRL 2 comes running from the theater.

                         GIRL 2
                    Olivia!

                         OLIVIA
                    Yes?

Girl 2 stares blankly. She can't find the words
to say.

                         GIRL 3
                    Out with it! Jesus.
                    You look like you're
                    about to have a coro-
                    nary.

                         GIRL 2
                    It's Jake!- His fami-
                    ly!

                         GIRL 3
                    Yeah, they found him.

                         GIRL 2
                    No!

Girl 2's fear-stricken voice has taken Girl 3's
careless facade taken down a notch.

                         GIRL 3
                    Well spit it out.

                         GIRL 2
                    Jake's parents were
                    murdered!

As the second girl relays the details, Olivia's
guilt over Jake's death is subsided. She's con-
fronted with everything he became. It's silly
to mourn over him now.
                         GIRL 3
                    Jesus, Olivia.- Are

                           155

you alright? You look
like you're in shock.

                    OLIVIA
          I think- I need to go
          home.

                    GIRL 3
          Are you sure?

Olivia nods.

                    OLIVIA
          I'll see you in class
          on Monday.

Olivia walks over to her car.

A young boy holds his scraped knee on a curb
near her car.

She ignores the crying boy as his friends are
there to help him already.

I/E. ANDOVER HIGH SCHOOL - PARKING LOT - CON-
TINUOUS

OLIVIA opens the back car seat and sees LIAM
staring wide-eyed.

She tosses the bags of blood to him and he
drinks them vigorously.

                    OLIVIA
          Are you alright?

                    LIAM
          That damn kid was the
          last straw. That would
          just be my luck.

                    OLIVIA
          You're telling me.-

Liam slows his pace, as she seems solemn.

                    LIAM
          What happened with
          you?
                    OLIVIA
          Oh- I just-. -It took
          me a while because
          the school was closed
          and they had a the-
          ater production go-
          ing on. Then I took
          little secret paths I
          learned from Jake when
          we were both in sum-
          mer school.- And then
          everything that could
          have gotten in my way
          just got in my way
          and- it was a lot.

Liam reaches out of the car to touch her hand.

                    LIAM
          Thank you, Olivia.-
          And don't blame your-
          self for what happened
          to Jake.

                    OLIVIA
          You see, I did for a
          bit, but- I just heard
          about what happened to
          his family.-

Liam withdraws his hand.

                    LIAM
          Are you sure you want
          to continue helping
          me?

                    OLIVIA
          Liam. Don't ask stupid
          questions. You're not
          to blame for Jake's
          death either.

She moves to close the seat again.

                    OLIVIA
          Come on. We have fami-
          ly to see.

EXT. RETIREMENT HOME - DRIVEWAY - DAY

OLIVIA and LIAM get out of the car and enter
the building.

INT. RETIREMENT HOME - LOBBY - CONTINUOUS

LIAM waits for the elevator and OLIVIA reads
her phone.

                    OLIVIA
          Oh God. I told you we
          should have gone home
          first.

                    LIAM
          We'll explain it to
          her later. This is im-
          portant.

INT. RETIREMENT HOME - COMMON AREA - LATER

Olivia's GREAT-GRANDMOTHER is staring off into
space.

LIAM approaches her slowly. This is the moment
he's been waiting for.

He stares at her blank expression and begins to
sings a lullaby in Gaelic words.

It's the tune his wife would sing to their
children long ago.

The old woman's face changes.

Slowly, she begins smiling.

Her eyes well up.

She sings along with him.

Liam stops, and she continues the song without him.

OLIVIA looks on with her GRANDMOTHER.

The great-grandmother finishes the tune, full of delight.

>   LIAM
>   Miss,- do you mind
>   telling me- where'd
>   you learn that song?

The old lady looks at him with a proud smile.

>   GREAT-GRANDMOTHER
>   My momma!

INT. RETIREMENT HOME - COMMON AREA- LATER

LIAM and OLIVIA are in deep conversation to-gether.

>   OLIVIA
>   I can take you.

>   LIAM
>   No, I've put you out
>   too much already.

>   OLIVIA
>   How do you plan to get
>   to Europe without me?

>   LIAM
>   I'll find a way.

>   OLIVIA
>   You'll need help.

>   LIAM
>   What about your moth-
>   er?

                    OLIVIA
          Telling her is for me
          to figure out.

A door swings open.

They look, and it's PATRICIA at the front door.

                    OLIVIA (Cont'd)
          You have a family,
          Liam. And if Lilly is
          still out there, she
          needs us too. You're
          not alone anymore.

Liam looks at Patricia as she speaks to the
WOMAN at the front counter.

Olivia is right. He can't afford to slip away
again.

                    OLIVIA
          Wait here. I'll intro-
          duce you to my mom.

Olivia runs over to her mother.

                    PATRICIA
          Who was over our
          house? And who is
          that?

                    OLIVIA
          Mom, I can explain ev-
          erything-

Liam looks on from a distance, unable to hear
what Olivia says.

Patricia's cold look changes. She looks at him
with curiosity; then the warmth reserved for
family.

Olivia waves him to come over.

Liam composes himself. It's another difficult introduction.

He steps forward, into the light of the front entrance. Beginning his walk toward an uncertain future.

Fade to black.

Afterword

Well, how was that?

I'm sorry about all the blood and unsettling scenes.

This story came to mind when a certain vampire series came out. It harped on the romantic ideas of vampires, making them "*cool*" and "*lusty*".

I wanted to make us fear vampires again; and after reading Dracula I was even more fired up to do something about it. Heavy influences come from the Korean movies and other foreign films I'd watch with my friends back in high school.

So let's get to business.

Let's talk about endings.

The original version of this story had Liam passing on to the next world and Olivia living out the rest of her life having been touched by her interaction with this long lost ancestor. A compelling art-house ending, but let's face it; it's not realistic by any means.

The old ending lived in my head until this past year, meaning a decade and a half of Liam dying was on my mind. Why change it?

When Liam's influence goes beyond a vampire and into the status of "*family member*", we can't just let him go like that. The audience has been on this journey after all, and Liam has become THEIR long-lost ancestor. We can't kill off their family member if it's not serving a narrative purpose other than "*woah, that was heavy*".

Another interesting effect of having Liam survive is, it plays against a trope us older viewers are used to. The trope goes "*If the character has done something horrible, they must sacrifice themselves to save the day. Otherwise we can't accept the film*".

It's not that much of a spoiler to put it this way, but *K-Pop Demon Hunters* has this trope; and by using an emotion we all sadly know, (loving someone who has lost their kindness and humanity to addiction) we can craft a new ending to this trope; therefore surprising our more seasoned viewers in a way that remains satisfying.

162

This change coincides with another change that happened within the past year; Liam used to be the main character.

By changing the main character to Olivia, we get less "*cool vampire story*" and more of a soul searching journey. It also allows for some mystery. Like the shark in Jaws, it's what we can't see that makes us so interested. Just like the set design in *The Lord of the Rings* movies; it's not telling us everything, but there's something there. It's telling us that there's more beyond the edges of the screen. We can ponder and discover more and more as we lie awake at night and wonder about "*that one thing*" that was never fully described in the movie.

To go back to the soul-searching: making Olivia the main character makes her less of a vessel for us to live through (*like some other vampire stories*) and makes her someone who NEEDS to grow. She NEEDS a character arc.

There are two arcs to take into consideration here: the *literal* arc of what PHYSICALLY happens on the screen, and the *character* arc: the emotionally motivating factors that change a character fundamentally.

A cheap emotional experience (*like a character death without a purpose*) will not fill us with the everlasting sensation that stories are SUPPOSED to give us. We need a permanent change in our character that we can follow and empathize with.

A main character death at the end of a story fits the narrative of a "*Greek Tragedy*" like *Oedipus* (*one of those "so-and-so many stories" we always hear about*), but the hallmark of a Greek Tragedy is an original sin, and Liam doesn't have one worth killing him over. His sins are his love for his daughter and his cravings. That's just not killable.

Olivia, on the other hand, can have a "*Coming of Age*" arc; and while that's a "*so-and-so many stories*" term, it's really just Pandora's Box for our story. We can light the fuse and make it less about "*what happens*" and more about "*how*" it happens.

It also helps to obscure the story type by leading as a "*Murder-Mystery*" and ending in the "*Coming of Age*" zone. In fact, something really fascinating to help you on your journey is to recognize what attracts us to media, and that's contrast. Contrasting expectations to outcomes makes for a unique story. Yes we have that "*so-and-so many stories*" but we've expanded that. Contrast is what makes us look at landscapes and recognize them as "*beautiful*". It's the contrast of color, of light; heck, that's even how we give the illusion of a picture on a piece of paper. It's just contrast on two-dimensions that we recognize as something "*beautiful*". Contrast in characters is key (*someone who is awesome in one way yet tumultuously flawed in another way*). Some favorite contrasting characters include Vegeta from *DragonBall Z*, any character from *Metal Gear*, *Batman*, and so many more. Contrast is everything in art; and it works for characters, their interactions in the story, and much more.

To loop back to the subject of story structure, let's take a smaller part of the story. Let's talk about Mrs. Krafton's fake-out "*death*" at the end. What was that about?

Well, I'm the writer so I'll tell you, it's a deliberate red-herring to make you think this is a comic-relief death (*Mrs. Krafton*) leading to the mentor death (*of Liam*). You know what I mean? Dumbledore and Gandalf and how they died in their respective stories? And think about Gandalf. Was he officially dead?

This is a "*trope*" and it's best when it's played to its maximum advantage. The term "*subversion*" refers to taking an expectation and knee-capping everything the viewer expected. The shock makes for an everlasting memory. Your brain logs it into the long-term memory vaults for survival purposes. You NEED to believe Liam WILL die. (*In other words, those seasoned viewers I mentioned before need to believe it's the same trope playing out again. We need to deliver the idea that he's done things too horrible to justify him surviving*). Only then can we get the weight of what this fakeout means to us. (Physically: He's found a lead! | Emotionally: God doesn't give up on us that easily.)

Let me phrase this in another way to make it extra clear because it's easy to read a book like this and look at these ideas as "*rules*" but they're more-so guidelines or terminology used in conversations about story structure. Having a clear definition to these terms is helpful, but we've all heard them misused a million times by viewers who have just walked out of the theater; so let me clarify one major misunderstanding.

What I mentioned earlier about a "*story-type*" change is a matter of using "*tropes*" to change the trajectory of the plot.

The story is set up as a murder-mystery (*the plot*) with all the tropes of that genre playing out. The "*plot thickens*" (*the word "**plot**" again*)

164

when it is revealed that one of the murders was committed by an ancestor of our main character; a vampire who's been alive for roughly 300 years. (*Building contrast in the plot to thicken it, and building contrast in character to give them "characterization"*).

THEN, Liam brings the investigative aspect to the murders, and the ex-boyfriend is introduced. He gets in trouble, regrets are mentioned, and if he's alive, there's potential for healing between Olivia and Jake. Heck, some people might hope they get back together.

We find the murderer and it's Arcturus. Jake is there. The old Roman vampire is killed. Jake is saved! Then… (*plot*)-twist!

THAT is a plot twist. It's not a random act of deus-ex-machina.

A plot twist is leading the audience down one path only to make things more interesting with an unexpected journey down another path. It appears as an unexpected reveal (*that we're going down a different path*) and so it's frequently confused for being "*an unexpected outcome*".

The question becomes "*Is the new path more interesting than the original path?*". That's where you make your decision, and you should choose the trajectory that is more interesting in your opinion.

The writers of South Park, Trey Parker and Matt Stone, have noted that stories need to be composed in a way that says (*and I'm paraphrasing here*) "*this happens, and THEREFORE, this happens, BUT, this happens, and THEREFORE, this.*" Trey goes on to say (*again, paraphrasing*) that if your story says "this happens and then this happens", you're screwed. (*Again, you'll notice these changes in trajectory generate* **contrast**).

A lot of professionally made stories have had underwhelming turn-outs (*even with incredible concepts*), and you might wonder how in the world that happens among professionals. The truth may shock you.

(*Not really, it's actually much more simple than that.*)

If there's anything a person will learn by the time they reach thirty, it's that nobody knows what the hell they're doing. I'm technically supposed to put you under an illusion that I'm some master storyteller. That's what "*branding*" would tell me to do; and technically, I'd be serving myself best by making sure you're a mindless consumers of what I make… but I'm a selfish lunatic who wants to see good stories and I need people to make those stories; so I'm going to tell you, I'm surprised by new things every day and that's natural. This is true for

165

any professional.

An eighth grade teacher I had told me about his ninety-year-old friend who confessed "I'm almost a century old and I'm still learning new things every day!"

For a lot of people this is scary. It's a Lovecraftian look into the infinite void of knowledge and paralyzes them with fear. It makes sense to feel this way at a first glance but it's silly upon further inspection.

I look at it as an adventure that never ends. Haven't we all read a book or watched a series that we just wished wouldn't end?

Life is an ongoing adventure with endless possibilities, it's not a scary abyss; and nothing makes a series more interesting than a good cliffhanger. We're all promised one of those.

The last piece of personal information I'd like to tell you about is my study process.

At a producer's conference I attended at Universal Studios, I won some raffle at an IMDB-Pro table. They offered me multiple prizes to choose from. A travel mug, a hat, a t-shirt, a notebook, etc.

I took one look and said "*I don't have any space in my cabinet for a mug. I can't fit another t-shirt in my drawer, and my girlfriend will KILL me if my pile of hats gets any larger; but I can never have enough of these!*" and I grabbed the notebook.

I have an endless mound of notebooks.

Everyone's process is different, so this isn't a demand, it's just my advice, but:

Taking hand-written notes has been scientifically proven to result in better long-term memory retention. Always take hand-written notes and try to organize them as best as you can. I have one book for story outlines, one for musings on certain stories and themes, another for lessons I think are applicable for future stories, and so-on.

Second, I always buy physical copies of the books that I study. The reason is similar to the notebooks. I keep sticky-notes on the pages so I can reference them later. It makes the ideas more uniform and organized and I'll have the pages right there along with the notes. These notes can be abbreviated in one of my notebooks with a numbering system (*sometimes even color-coded if I have the luxury*) so I can see the numbered note (*in my notebook*) and match it with the numbered *sticky*note extending from the source's pages.

Third, the mentality of all of this is important (*as mentioned in the foreword*). This goes for anything in life. If you're stressing about things, it doesn't mean you should give up on it. It doesn't mean "*lose sleep over it*" either. It means you need to slow down and ask yourself why you're so stressed. Ask yourself "*how can I make this as easy as breathing?*"

If you can listen to YouTube videos, Audiobooks, or Podcasts while you cook, clean, or anything else that requires absolutely no brainpower, then do it. Make it as easy as breathing. Get creative in killing two birds with one stone. You'll thank me later, and you'll be looking with anticipation at the long journey, rather than dreading the unfathomable void. Just always think:

"As easy as breathing."

So what's the deal? Why is this book so short if it's full of direction and help on writing?

Easy. People have written plenty on it, and I'm just going to guide you to the right books.

These tid-bits I've given here are relevant to the story you've just read and you can come back to the story any time you'd like once you've studied the craft. We all have screenplays we study (*I even have a photocopy of the original Star Wars*) and you can consider this your first screenplay to put into your library of stories to study.

The rest of what I'll tell you is further reading and resources for your journey as a writer

Okay, so here's the crucial part. What to read? What to watch? What to listen to?

Let's start with the books because clearly you're a reader:

"On Writing" by Stephen King. It's mostly about writing form the perspective of a novelist and its topics can be quite different for that reason, but it's still applicable for screenplay writers.

Next, we have the essential writing books for filmmakers:

"*Story*" by Robert McKee, "*Save The Cat*" by Blake Snyder, "*Anatomy of a Story*" by John Truby, and last but not least (*I just dug through my library to find this paperback copy of a book that's missing its cover*), "Break Into Screenwriting" by Ray Frensham (*or "Raymond Frensham" according to Goodreads*).

The first three books mentioned here are almost cliché to mention because everyone and their mother has read them in Hollywood.

I would start with "*Story*" by McKee first. He's humble enough to mention that his words aren't supposed to be followed to the T. Snyder on the other hand seems to think there's only a handful of ways to save a cat and it's soulless to look at things that way. Not to say he's got bad advice; in fact he has excellent information on writing that should not be overlooked just because of his know-it-all attitude.

Next, there's some unusual reading (*for screenwriters*) that I'd highly recommend because it's best to have cohesion between different professions. The final picture (*and therefore your work*) will look better if you do your part to streamline the process of making the movie. This isn't your project (*and nobody else's for that matter*), so don't get an ego. In reality, the film is the final product of everyone's hard work, with the goal of maximizing the experience for the audience. In other words, you're looking to make an enjoyable film that you can be proud to TAKE PART in making. I don't care if people tout the greatness of "*this director or that*". **All of us** know we'd be nothing without our teams.

"Non-writing" books about filmmaking:
First, there's "*In the Blink of an Eye*" by Walter Murch. This is the essential "*editor's book*". Murch is a master of this craft, which has been called "sculpting in time" by Andrei Tarkovsky; and as such, Murch is responsible for sculpting many of our favorite moments in cinema.

Next, I'd recommend "*Creativity Inc.*" by Ed Catmull. It's a great way to see the inner workings of a creative process, and it will likely make you feel at ease to see how human people are in the creative world. Also (and I can't stress this enough) it expresses the importance of "*candor*". A crucial thing that a lot of people struggle with, and Ed Catmull explains this better than anyone else.

And I think that's all for now. Your hands will be full with all that for the time being, and I'll leave other recommendations for the future (*if anyone cares to know more*).

Setting aside the story craft conversation, I think that an understanding of business and finance is crucial for filmmakers. I hate to say it because I love the idea of artsy-fartsy filmmakers doing their thing and being revered for it; but to be honest, if you make the wrong move and don't abide by the law as it's practiced, you could get sued (*maybe even go to jail in rare cases*). Nobody will distribute your project if there's a legal issue in the production of your film. They don't want to be sued and they don't want to buy something that they can't distribute.

A friend of mine recently landed a distribution deal after navigating a major headache. He had no idea where the finances for his film came from. The producer sourced the finances from a bunch of friends and the filmmaker had no idea what was agreed upon in these negotiations. He then had to track down release forms; getting written permission for each cast member and location. To do this retroactively is a massive headache. Learn the legal and business side and you'll be a lot happier for doing it; BUT ALSO... don't be afraid to mess up. Do your due-diligence and learn as much as you can, but failure is the best teacher. Again, all of us have failed. All of us have had a moment where we had no idea what we were doing. Anyone who pretends they know everything is putting on a facade for their own personal "*branding*". I've had to wade through a cesspool of stupidity to get this information to you, just know that you'll have to wade through your fair-share of nonsense too.

A good place to start is: look up LLCs, S-Corps, sole proprietorships, and so-on. You can mitigate your risks by researching that extensively.

I'd like to talk more about this here, but rather than boring you with text, I think I'll start posting interviews with friends of mine on social media. There's people I've learned a lot from, and I've always wanted to have an excuse to link up with them.

These are good friends of mine with extensive experience as producers, writers, and artists in multiple major studios around Hollywood. I can't package their wisdom in a short book. An interview posted online would cost less for you anyway.

Now, outside of reading, where can you learn more about writing? The short answer: YouTube.

"*Hello Future Me*", "*Trope Talk*" from Overly Sarcastic Productions, and "*Terrible Writing Advice*" are some of the best resources I'd listen to while doing dishes and other mundane tasks. I've recently found a channel called "*The Second Story*" and I think it's an excellent resource as well.

Also, I used to play "*The Elder Scrolls IV: Oblivion*" while listening

169

to Stephen King's "*On Writing*" and it was my "*relaxing time*". I rented "*On Writing*" through an app called "Hoopla" by connecting it with my library card. Again, the physical copy was a place for my sticky notes so I could go back and reference my notes at any time rather than going "*What was that part again?*" and scrubbing through a multiple hour timeline of information.

The content in this book, both before and after the script, are just an introduction to the world of story craft. One day, I'd like to make a more extensive book about the process of creativity, but that would take a long time.

For now, all I can offer is some small insights through social media channels. You can find me at the places listed below and follow the status of my future projects on these platforms:

Instagram: @erikjamestroy
X: @ChilliumWalrus

Social media accounts linked to my novel "*Icarus Dawns*" can be found here:

Instagram: @icarusdawns
YouTube: @IcarusDawns
X: @IcarusDawns

And finally, I am making a movie!

Calameda Road is a comedy / action / thriller about an armored truck driver and comic book enthusiast named Trevor who grew up without a father, his mother passed away last year, and he's been struggling with his personal health; but when his armored truck becomes the target of a heist (*at the hands of some misfit robbers and their demented ringleader*), he needs to look within himself and find his inner hero to survive.

More about this story can be found at these links on social media:

Instagram: @CalamedaRoad
YouTube: @CalamedaRoad

I will also provide a QR code below if you'd like to become a part of

170

the emailing list to stay informed about current and future projects.

Thank you for taking the time to read this story and I hope my research has been helpful for you. I look forward to sharing more in the future and until then, happy writing!